THE
FRINGE OF
GOLD

THE FRINGE·OF GOLD

THE FISHING VILLAGES
OF SCOTLAND'S EAST COAST,
ORKNEY & SHETLAND

CHARLES MACLEAN

CANONGATE
1985

Acknowledgements

Without the help and advice of a great number
of people — in local museums and libraries, in
bars and on quaysides — this book would be
hopelessly inadequate to the task we set for it.

It is impossible to list them, but the author and
his research assistant would like to acknowledge
and thank them all.

We would also like, especially, to thank John
Hutchison of the Scottish Tourist Board,
without whom . . .

First published in 1985
by Canongate Publishing Ltd.
17 Jeffrey Street, Edinburgh.

© Charles MacLean 1985

*The publishers acknowledge the financial assistance
of the Scottish Tourist Board in the
publication of this volume.*

Research Assistant, **Alison Rae**
Cover painting, **James Howie**

British Library Cataloguing in Publication Data
   MacLean, Charles, 1946—
    The fringe of gold; the fishing villages of Scotland's
    East coast, Orkney and Shetland.
    1. Fishing villages—Scotland—History
    2. Scotland—Social life and customs
    I. Title
    94.1   DA772

   ISBN 0 86241 061 4

Illustration on Page 40 by
Alyson MacNeil
Alyson MacNeil

Illustration on Page 78
by **Alasdair Gray**

Illustrations on Pages 4 and 5
by **Roger Finch**

Illustrations on Pages 28, 43 and 89
by **Peter F. Anson**

Printed and bound by
Smith Print Group, Newcastle upon Tyne

Photographs kindly supplied by
Aberdeen Maritime Museum
Aberdeen University Library
Kirkcaldy Museums and Art Gallery
Dundee District Libraries
D. C. Thomson & Co., Dundee
Charles Tait Photographic, Orkney
The Scottish Fisheries Museum Trust Ltd.,
Anstruther.

FOR JAMES HOWIE,
ARTIST OF AUCHMITHIE,
WHO FIRST INTRODUCED
ME TO THE FISHING
VILLAGES OF THE
EAST COAST.

CONTENTS

Foreword 1

Introduction 2
History, Tradition and Superstition — Fishing Craft and Fishing Methods

THE NORTHERN MAINLAND AND THE ISLES
Voe — Vidlin — Lunna — Mossbank — Sullom Voe — Graven — Ollaberry — Collafirth —
North Roe — Stenness — Ronas Voe — Heylor — Gloup — Whalfirth — Cullivoe —
Mid Yell — Unst — Uyeasound — Baltasound — Haroldswick — Norwick — Burrafirth

Bibliography 114

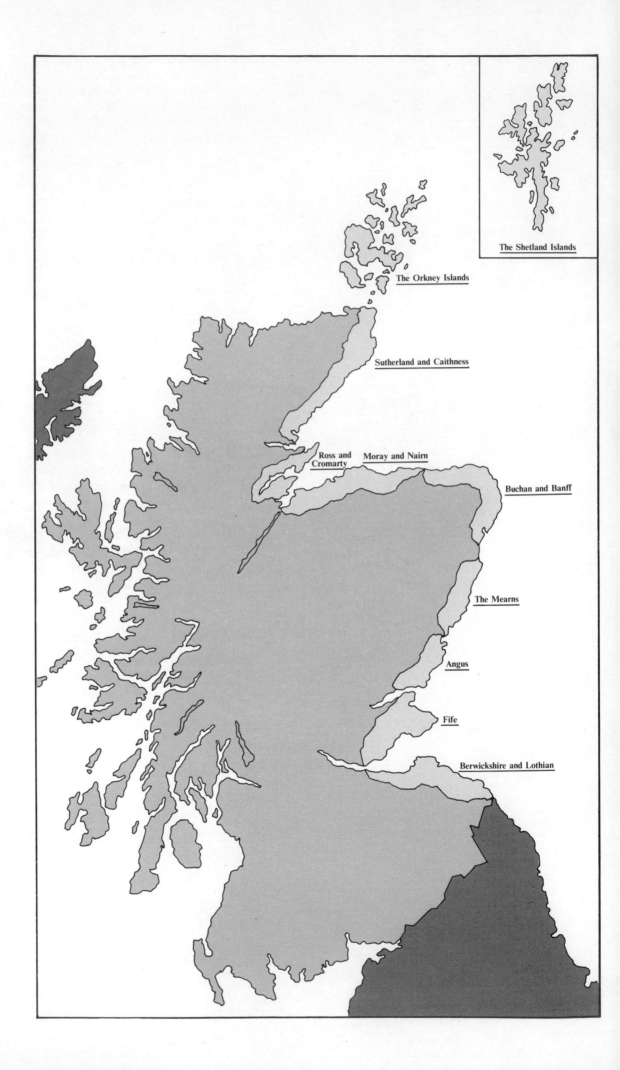

The Shetland Islands

The Orkney Islands

Sutherland and Caithness

Ross and
Cromarty   Moray and Nairn

Buchan and Banff

The Mearns

Angus

Fife

Berwickshire and Lothian

James VI (1567-1625) described his kingdom of Scotland as 'A beggar's mantle fringed with gold'. The fringe he was referring to was the coast of Fife — still today a string of jewel-like villages; then a series of important ports, trading with Northern Europe and 'pursuing the fishing'. It is fanciful to suppose that, were the King of Scots alive today he would apply the same term to his kingdom, yet 'The Fringe of Gold' still seems to me an apt description of our eastern seaboard.

Between the border and John O'Groats are 135 coastal towns, villages and hamlets which owe their existence to fishing. Time has been kind to almost all of them: the fishers' cottages built in 1900, or 1850 or 1750, still stand — perhaps embellished with dormer windows or pebble-dash, and certainly more comfortable inside, but otherwise the same as they were when the fishing was at its height.

The quays and piers are heavy with memories; the focus of the communities they serve. Wonderfully wrought and marvellously worn by the sea, they stand like noble sculptures, monuments to the generations for whom they have provided safe harbours. And everywhere there are traces of the past — rusting winches on the boat-strand beaches, ancient barometers at the pierhead, boats built in 1900 and still in service — all the evocative detritus of the sea.

Yet the villages of the East Coast are by no means only shrines to a past way of life. Over 60 per cent of the fish landed in the United Kingdom is landed there: fishing is still done from almost all of them, though on a reduced scale, and where the harbours are too small to handle modern boats, the fishermen travel to the major ports for work. There are boatbuilders and fish processors, markets and chandlers, fish merchants and curers, as well as craft shops and cottage industries and modern facilities for visitors which include a number of excellent small museums devoted to the way of life of the fisherfolk.

Every village is different and each has its own charm as well as its own story. It is beyond the scope of this book to give more than an introduction to them and a glimpse of their history and customs, but if it can introduce its readers to the beauty and interest of a largely overlooked part of Scotland, it will have served its purpose.

Maclean

Charles MacLean,
Kildonan,
Isle of Arran.
March 1985.

History It is possible that the East Coast of Scotland was inhabited earlier than any other part of the British Isles, and it is likely that from a very remote time fishing was pursued from these shores by coastal farmers. This pattern — fishing during the summer months and farming as well — remained the same for thousands of years, and until modern times most of the communities on the East Coast were crofting hamlets. Small open boats with single lug-sails were hauled up onto the beach when not at sea, and the men pursued haddock, cod and ling with hook and line. The fish were sold fresh in the neighbourhood, and any surplus was either carried further inland for sale or cured by drying, salting or smoking.

The first systematic support for fishing came from the Church. In cathedral towns like Arbroath the monks encouraged full-time fishing by buying the entire catch and distributing it to the poor, and also by supporting the fisherfolk during lean seasons. Government involvement first occurred during the reign of James II (1460-88) when the Crown began to offer bounties (i.e. cash rewards) and other incentives, and during the following 300 years harbours were built and fishing encouraged in a variety of ways, so that by the middle of the 18th century there were established communities of fisherfolk up and down the entire coast.

Haddock and cod was, and still is, the principal catch, and until the late 18th century little attempt was made to catch the shoals of herring that appeared off the east coast at certain times of the year. The Dutch successfully fished herring with drift nets, but Scots fishermen did not have boats equipped to catch or transport the fish, nor the means to process and preserve it, and they did not have access to markets in which they could sell the short-lived glut of herring.

Then, in the 1790s, merchants and curers in Caithness set up a contract system with the fishermen for the supply of herring, and established pickling and curing sheds to handle the catches. By 1800 over 200 boats were involved in the two-month season and from 1808 the industry expanded rapidly, until all the main ports on the south coast of the Moray Firth had also mobilised themselves for the herring fishery. By 1820 there were a thousand boats congregating in the Moray Firth for the season and as the century advanced the numbers continued to grow, until the industry became the greatest fishery in Europe.

The principal market for pickled herring was initially Ireland and the West Indies, where the fish was fed to the slaves, but after the Napoleonic War enormous markets on the continent of Europe and Russia were opened up.

At the peak of the 'herring boom' in 1907, 2,500,000 barrels of fish, weighing over a quarter of a million tons, were cured and exported, over two-thirds of it going to Germany, Eastern Europe and Russia: in 1913 there were 10,000 boats involved in the Scottish herring industry.

The Fisher Lassies

Throughout the herring boom Scots fisher-lassies were a famous sight at any of the ports where herring were landed.

These girls came from fishing villages all round the coast of Scotland and began gutting and packing the 'silver darlings' at the age of 15, taught by older sisters and friends. Throughout the season they travelled with the fish — from Stornoway to Lerwick to Peterhead to Yarmouth — all their possessions packed in a small wooden chest, which also served as a chair, table and wardrobe in the unfurnished wooden huts that were their accommodation. They worked and lived in teams of three, two gutters and a packer.

The work was arduous and the conditions hard, yet the girls were proud of their calling, looked forward to the season each year and had a reputation for tremendous good humour and quick wit. As can be imagined, they were very popular with the fishermen, who would banter with them as they worked in the hope of being invited to tea on Sundays, the only day the girls had off. Most girls met their future husbands in this way, and thereafter gave up the travelling life.

The daily routine was as follows: the girls were woken at 5 a.m. by a cooper banging on the door and calling, 'Get up and tie your fingers!' Over a cup of tea they tied up their fingers with cotton bandages made out of flour bags: if they nicked themselves with their sharp gutting knives the wound would quickly turn septic and they would have to go home. Since they gutted and packed 60 or 70 herrings a minute, the chance of this was high.

Work depended on the amount of fish landed: if there was a large catch they worked late into the night. They started at 6 a.m.; breakfasted on porridge, bread and jam at 8.30 a.m.; ate a hot lunch (soup, mince, tatties and doughboys followed by suet pudding was very popular; the food was prepared the night before); and, if there was not too much work on, they were back in their huts for a tea of herrings and scones or pancakes at 6 p.m.

The herrings were first dumped in large open troughs called 'farlins', where they received an initial salting. With one stroke of the knife the girls removed head and gut and transferred the fish to a smaller tub, grading it by size at the same time, where it was more thoroughly salted. The packer then laid out the herrings in a barrel — packing them in tightly, with alternate layers at different angles: the test for a well-packed barrel was that the layers of fish remained in place even when the cask was removed.

By this time the industry was no longer seasonal or local. The boats followed the shoals clockwise around the coast of Britain, and with the boats travelled an army of fisher-lassies, curers, coopers, merchants and general hands. In the spring the shoals were in the Minch, in the early summer Shetland, in the summer and early autumn in the north-east and in the late autumn off East Anglia. Some years there was also a late fishery off the Isle of Man and the west coast of Ireland.

There were three distinct herring seasons, and many fishermen took part in all three, following the fish according to the time of year.

The Winter Herring (January, February and March) were mainly found in the Forth and at Wick. The Summer Herring (June, July and August) were pursued up the whole of the East Coast as far as Shetland.

The English and Irish Fishing (September, October and November), when boats and curers would travel to Grimsby and Lowestoft, or to the West of Ireland.

White fish (haddock and cod) could be caught all year round: during the winter months the fishermen worked 'sma' lines' close to shore; during the summer many of them would sail further afield and fish 'great lines'.

After the Russian Revolution in 1917 the Russian market for herring collapsed, and in the years following World War I, the Germans, Norwegians and Dutch began to develop their own fishing industry. At home the Depression raged through the post-war decade and a half, equipment was more expensive — and most of it was out of date — and running costs rose. By 1934 the herring catch was less than half that of 1913. The herring fleet rapidly diminished and the industry became concentrated on a handful of larger ports like Peterhead and Fraserburgh.

The modern Scottish fishing industry is greatly trimmed down from its 1913 peak. There are about 9,000 active fishermen working about 2,000 boats, backed by nearly 25,000 shore workers. Nevertheless it is still a very important economic force: over 60 per cent of the UK fish catch is landed in Scotland, worth about £150 million, and 90 per cent of it was brought in by Scottish boats in 1983.

Although the boats tend to congregate in about 20 ports, and although the huge majority of fish is landed at Peterhead, Fraserburgh and Aberdeen, many fishermen still live in the villages of their ancestors, driving to and from the harbour where their boat is based. Thus — quite apart from the amount of lobster and crab fishing, small boat line-fishing and light net fishing that is done from many of the harbours today — the smaller villages on the East Coast are still 'fishing communities' in the fullest sense of the word.

Traditions and Superstitions

The fishing communities developed their own customs, traditions and folklore; they were tight-knit and conservative. They regarded outsiders, especially farmers, with suspicion and often with hostility, and their names, food, mode of life, dress, even dialect, was different from the surrounding country. It was rare for them to marry outwith their own community.

They were an unusually superstitious class of people, perhaps because of the hazardous nature of their occupation; possibly because 'these see the works of the Lord and his wonders in the deep'. There were unlucky words ('minister', 'kirk', 'rabbit', 'rat', 'salmon', 'pig' and 'salt' were the most common) and even unlucky surnames (Ross, Coull, Campbell, Duffus, Anderson). If the men encountered a hare, a dog, a person with red hair or flat feet, or a minister, they were likely to refuse to put to sea; and if a rabbit, hare, dove, pigeon, or pig was found aboard the boat they certainly would not set out. Several birds were regarded as bringers of good or bad luck: curlews were called the 'Seven Whistlers' and were a sure omen of death and shipwreck; seagulls embody the souls of dead fishermen; swallows and wild geese flying out to sea meant good weather.

'Wild geese, wild geese, gangin t' the sea,
Good weather it will be.
Wild geese, wild geese, gangin t' the hill,
The weather it will spill.'

Horseshoes were often nailed to the mast for luck, or sprigs of rowan tied to the lines or rowlocks to avert the Evil Eye. Herring scales were never washed from the deck. Sometimes crews would take with them a length of wool or thread tied with three magic knots by a 'wise woman': if a light breeze was wanted the first knot would be untied; if a strong breeze, the second; the final knot must not be unfastened or a gale would ensue.

There were superstitions relating to the building, launching and rigging of boats; observances required during the 'redding' (preparing) of lines and nets; words that should, or should not, be spoken as the nets were shot or hauled in. There were initiation ceremonies before a boy could become a fisherman; curious marriage customs; special funeral observances, like the one in some villages on the Moray Firth where, if a fisherman was lost at sea, the community gathered together, collected as much food and drink as they could muster, and went to inform the man's widow in a body, carrying with them all that would be required for the wake.

Until modern times custom and superstition influenced every aspect of a fisherman's life, and echoes of the old ways are still found in the villages today.

**Fishing Craft
and
Fishing Methods**

Until 1855 none of the fishing boats on the East Coast of Scotland had any decking; they were entirely open and of an average length of only 20 feet. As early as the 15th century attempts had been made by the Crown to encourage the building of larger, decked boats which could work further from land, and in the reign of James III (1460-88) all maritime burghs were required to build 'great ships, busses, pink boats with nets and all other necessities of fishing'. Due to lack of funding the scheme floundered. From mediaeval times to the end of the 18th century fishing in the North Sea was monopolised by the Dutch, who, early on, had employed heavy **'busses'** to work offshore. These were about 80 feet in length, with a 15-foot beam; initially three-masted and square-rigged on each mast. The fore and main masts could be lowered into crutches when the ship was lying head to the wind, riding to her nets.

The boats used by coastal fishermen during the same period developed into three types:

2. From Wick to the southern shore of the Moray Firth the **Scaffie** was favoured. These boats were between 20 and 40 feet in length, had a curved stem and a very sharply raked stern, and were rigged with one or two masts (sometimes even three on the largest vessels). The smaller scaffies were referred to as 'yawls', a term which echoes 'yole' rather than referring to the boat's rig.

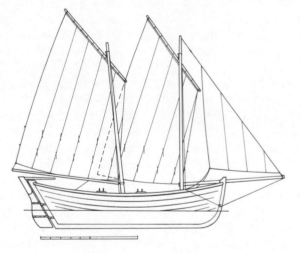

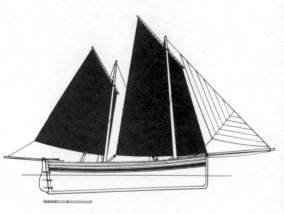

1. The **North Isles Yole** was developed in Orkney and used mainly in the far north. The boat was double-ended (pointed at both bow and stern) and raked fore and aft — a reminder of Orkney's long connections with the vikings. The average length of a yole was 19 feet and her beam was about 9 feet — an unusual 2:1 ratio which made plenty of room for gear — and they were generally rigged with two standing lug-sails and a jib.

3. Between Aberdeen and Eyemouth the more heavily built **Fifie** was the boat most commonly used. Both stem and stern of these boats were almost vertical, and they tended to be built larger than the scaffies — up to 65 feet overall.

Until 1855 neither Fifies nor Scaffies were decked — it was considered essential for herring fishing that the boats be open — and it took the example of the R.N.L.I. who built and successfully worked a decked Scaffie, to persuade fishermen of the desirability of a partly decked boat which was very much safer in heavy weather.

In 1879 the marriage between a boatbuilder from Lossiemouth and a fisher-lass from Fife was sealed by the building of a boat which combined the finer characteristics of both the Fifie and the Scaffie. The **Zulu**, named after the war which finished that year, had a deep, straight

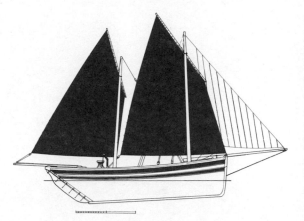

stem and a sharply raked stern. She was decked and rigged with an enormously high free-standing mainmast — set well forward — and a smaller mizzen. This meant that the decks were kept free of standing rigging, and it meant that the boat could carry an enormous area of canvas.

Within only a few years the Zulu design had been adopted for larger boats up and down the entire coast: they were built up to 75 feet in length, and have been described as the most noble sailing craft ever designed in Britain. "The sense of grandeur and power that they conveyed when reaching in a hard breeze has never been surpassed by any other craft under canvas" (Anson).

The boats of a community tended to be owned by family groups, each fisherman owning a share, and many groups owned more than one boat — a small one for inshore work and a larger one for offshore fishing. In autumn and winter the quarry tended to be inshore haddock and cod, caught on 'sma' lines'; in spring and summer the fishermen travelled further afield, catching cod and ling with 'great lines' or drift-netting for herring in season.

The first steam drifter built in Scotland appeared eight years before the first Zulu, but steam power was adopted only very slowly. Then, in 1882, a consortium of Aberdeen merchants purchased a steam tug, the *Toiler*, and converted her ' for the purpose of prosecuting trawl fishing' for white fish. At first, opposition to the new method was loud and the fishermen sceptical, but the project was an immediate and phenomenal success, and within a few years Aberdeen had become the foremost port in the country, with a fleet of over 200 **steam trawlers** fishing for cod and haddock far offshore and reaching the great fishing grounds of the northern North Sea.

Unlike drift-netting, trawling requires a boat which can raise a considerable turn of speed to drag the heavy net along the seabed, and for this reason it was an unsuitable method for the small sailing boats of the East Coast. However, since steam trawlers were so much bigger than even the largest Fifies and Zulus they could only be accommodated in a few harbours, and places where they congregated — like Aberdeen — tended to attract fishermen from neighbouring villages, so that fishing from these smaller places declined.

The large catches landed by the steam trawlers lowered the price of white fish and made it uneconomical to pursue line fishing. A certain amount was still done, however — even today line fishing is still pursued from Gourdon in Aberdeenshire — and with the introduction of the internal combustion marine engine in 1906, smaller boats again came into their own. Initially motor power was used as an auxiliary to sail power, but by the First World War there were as many **motor fishing vessels** as there were steam, and by the 1930s there were twice as many. The last steam trawler was built in 1927.

A great boost to motor power came with the introduction of the Danish seine-net in 1922, which needed only a small boat to work it, and about the same time the diesel engine was introduced.

Today there are still half a dozen yards on the East Coast either building fishing boats out of wood along traditional lines or finishing steel and ferro-cement hulls. The greater part of the Scottish fishing fleet is made up of vessels

East Coast Registration Marks

Every fishing boat carries a registration mark — usually painted on the bow — in the form of a number and letters. The letters are a code for the town of registration, but boats may well work out of a different harbour from their home port, and often move from place to place as the season, or the fishing, changes.

A	Aberdeen	INS	Inverness
AH	Arbroath	KY	Kirkcaldy
BF	Banff	LH	Leith
BK	Berwick	ME	Montrose
BCK	Buckie	PD	Peterhead
BU	Burntisland	WK	Wick
FR	Fraserburgh		

Steam Trawler

between 30 and 60 feet long — small in comparison to the boats built at the end of the last century, but even the smallest of them are equipped with the latest electronic aids to navigation and fish location. A larger boat — over 80 feet in length — can easily cost a million pounds when fully fitted out, and even the nets used today cost considerably more than an entire Zulu fishing boat: the great purse-seine nets which can encircle whole shoals, made out of lightweight synthetic fibre, cost around £100,000.

Methods of Fishing

1. **Sma' Line and Great Line**
   Until the arrival of the steam trawler in 1882, white fish (cod, haddock, ling etc.) was always caught by hook and line.
   Sma' lines were usually 300 feet long, and each had 100 'snoods' (little lines running off the main line), each with eight to ten hooks attached, baited with mussels or lugworms.
   Great lines were longer and heavier, being used in deeper water to catch larger fish (cod and halibut particularly) though they had only 80 hooks, baited with small haddock and herring.

2. **Stake Nets**
   Used for salmon fishing up and down the coast. A strip of netting is attached to upright stakes which are anchored at low tide in shallow water so as to form an enclosure with an opening facing out to sea. The fish enter at high tide and are unable to escape.

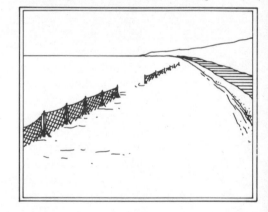

3. **Drift Net**
   The traditional method used for catching herring, the drift net is a long rectangular curtain, corked to float 12 feet below the surface of the sea, which caught the fish by the gills. At either end of the net is a buoy, and the bottom of the net is held down by a heavy rope, which is also used for hauling in the catch.
   Once the net has been shot, the drifter lowers her foremast and lies head to wind, drifting with the tide for two or three hours before hauling in the catch. Very little drift netting is done today.

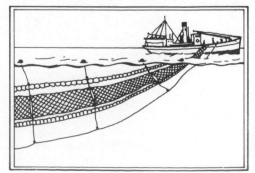

4. Trawling

Trawling for white fish (cod, haddock etc.) was only introduced to Scotland in 1882, but has been the principal method ever since.

The trawl net is a bag which is dragged along the sea bed. Its bottom edge rolling on great metal rollers or 'bobbins' and its mouth kept open by the pressure of the water against the 'otterboards' on either side.

The method has been adapted into a 'pair trawl', towed by two boats, to catch herring and mackerel. Since these fish swim shallower than white fish, the pair trawl net is lighter and is drawn through mid-water.

5. Seine Net

The seine net was introduced from Denmark in 1922. It is lighter than a trawl net, but, like the other, is a drag net, weighted along its bottom edge and corked along the top. The net is held open by the tide and is shot when the fishing boat is broadside on to the tidal flow.

The procedure for seine net fishing is different from trawling in that an anchor attached to a flag buoy is first heaved overboard. The boat then moves away from the marker, paying out line, until it is some distance 'downstream' when the net is shot. The boat returns to the buoy, completing a triangular course, picks it up and hauls in both lines simultaneously, gradually closing the bag of the net as it rises from the sea bed.

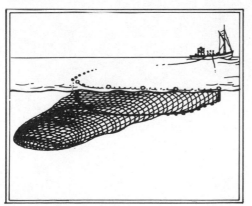

6. Purse-seine Net

The purse-seine is the principal method used today to catch pelagic fish (herring and mackerel). The nets are lightweight and enormous in extent — they can be as big as a football pitch — and they work on the principle of a draw-string purse. The net is spread below a shoal of fish and then hoisted to the surface, with the draw-strings tightening, trapping the catch as it surfaces.

BERWICKSHIRE
AND LOTHIAN

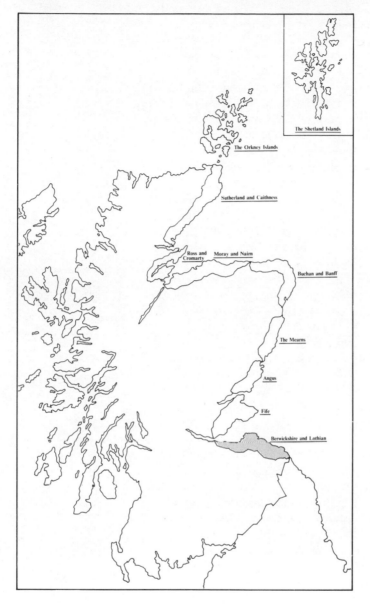

The Orkney Islands

The Shetland Islands

Sutherland and Caithness

Ross and
Cromarty

Moray and Nairn

Buchan and Banff

The Mearns

Angus

Fife

Berwickshire and Lothian

The eastern coastline as one crosses the Border into Scotland has been compared to that of Cornwall or Norway, or even Nova Scotia. The cliffs begin as steep braes and then become fearsome bulwarks of crimson sandstone towards, and round, St Abb's Head. After this the shoreline becomes gentler — sandy beaches interspersed with outcrops of rock — and flat arable farmland stretching away behind. Some of the villages in Berwickshire and Lothian are very ancient, and lying so close to Scotland's old enemy, England, suffered continual depredation at the hands of the invaders. The relative loneliness of the area, and the close trading links with Northern Europe enjoyed by the larger towns in days gone by also made smuggling a lucrative pastime for many of the communities.

The first villages encountered cling to the foot of steep cliffs at the end of a ravine. **Ross** and **Upper Burnmouth** are one community, though they developed as separate villages. Ross has no harbour, and in the old days the boats were dragged up the beach: the harbour at Burnmouth was built in 1830, enlarged in 1870 (when the W-shaped breakwater was constructed with a beacon at its end) and restored in 1959.

A visitor to the place in 1913 remarked that Burnmouth was entered 'round a great boulder', which lay at one end of the single street: the other end terminated in a cliff. Today, the boulder has disappeared and the row of cottages is approached by a rough track through the pebbles above the high water mark on the rocky beach. The way passes an ancient lifeboat shed and the remains of its ramp. The row of old rubble cottages which make up the village are the very same as those commented on by the 1913 traveller, with the difference that where he observed that they were 'all kept most scrupulously clean, the door steps ornamented with patterns that some suppose to have been handed down from mother to daughter from immemorial time', today they are mostly in poor condition. These original cottages are mostly holiday homes: the fishermen themselves all live in Upper Burnmouth.

In the mid-nineteenth century, white fish was sent from Burnmouth to Edinburgh every day by road, and live lobsters and crabs transported by sea to London: today the eight or nine boats working out of Burnmouth still make a living from their creels.

Eyemouth, with its harbour built around the sheltered mouth of the Eye Water, has been an important port — both for fishing and trade — since mediæval times. James VI made it a free port in 1597 which led, indirectly, to the place becoming a centre for smuggling in the eighteenth and nineteenth centuries.

The harbour we see today was originally

SMUGGLING

An immense contraband trade was carried on along the coast of Berwickshire, up to the turn of the nineteenth century; the precipitous cliffs, creeks and caves providing the essentials for successful 'free-trade'.

St Abb's Head was a favourite haunt of the smuggling fraternity, for whole cargoes of contraband could be smuggled away in the recesses of the great headland. The bay of Eyemouth, however, was the 'London Docks' for illicit trade in this district, its situation greatly facilitating the landing of goods. Wines, spirits, tea and tobacco were imported in large quantities and stored in the town houses, many of which were provided with cellars and secret caches when they were first built, expressly designed for this purpose.

Tradition has it that there were secret cellars and underground passages, secret cupboards and recesses in the thatched roofs, in all of which the 'free' imports were hidden. Eyemouth was described in 1927 as 'dark and cunning of aspect, full of curious alleys, blind and otherwise, and having no single house of any standing but what could unfold its tales of wonder'.

Smuggling was not an occupation exclusive to the poor; there is abundant evidence to show that the rich did much to facilitate business in contraband on a grand scale. There were gentlemen smugglers who no doubt financed the smuggling enterprises of the poorer folk.

There is, in Eyemouth, an old estate called Gunsgreen, the mansion house of which occupies a picturesque situation above the harbour. Today it is the headquarters of the local golf club, but it was built in the early years of the eighteenth century by a man who amassed a fortune in contraband trade and the house and outside offices are full of secret chambers. Over a hundred years ago when a field on the Gunsgreen estate was being ploughed, the earth suddenly gave way and the horses plunged into a pit which was found to be a vaulted subterranean chamber, a relic of smuggling days.

designed and built in 1768 by Smeaton, the greatest harbour architect of his time, who built large parts of Peterhead and Aberdeen harbours. It is built in such a way that the harbour mouth, which is only 150 feet wide, faces west, away from the prevailing wind and weather. In 1964 it was deepened and reconstructed, and today it is one of the best on the east coast, sheltering one of Scotland's largest trawling fleets, about fifty boats, though not all of them are based there full time.

There is an active fish market every day of the week except Sunday. Lobster tanks keep shellfish fresh, and behind the harbour are

Eyemouth

"There are no larger or
ner lug-sail boats on
he East Coast than
hose built at
yemouth, nor a
ardier or more
nterprising race of
shermen."
Archibald Young, 1884

'Salt' was a word
hat up until about
905 Berwickshire
ishermen avoided
sing while at sea.
A story is told that
n Eyemouth boat ran
hort of salt in the
utumn of 1905 when
shing. Hailing a
'armouth drifter, the
kipper called out: 'We
eed something that we
inna want tae speak
boot.' Whereupon the
nglish skipper shouted
ack- 'Is it salt ye
vant?' The salt was
anded over, but the
nglishmen remarked
hat all the rest of the
cottish crew had
isappeared below
ather than hear the
errible word spoken
n their presence.
Anson

traditional curing houses where fish is smoked. The long-established firm of William Weatherhead & Sons has specialised in building fishing boats for over a hundred years.

Eyemouth fishermen were a proud breed with many curious customs and traditions and their own costume.

In the 1850s the 'rig' of an Eyemouth fisherman consisted of a pair of loose-fitting blue serge breeches, tied at the knee with tapes, over which were pulled a thick pair of long woollen stockings reaching well over the knee. At sea he would wear a heavy pair of leather waders, and on shore leather slippers. A 'gansey' or Guernsey sweater (hand knitted on four needles and having no sewing anywhere) was worn on top and on his head he wore a blue bonnet, like a Tam O'Shanter, with a blue tassel. Towards the end of the century, the bonnet gave way to a straw boater with a glazed top, and early this century this was replaced by a little round sealskin cap. In earlier years a tall silk 'stovepipe' hat was the customary headgear ashore, worn at a rakish tilt and known as a 'rakie step'.

Young men had to endure an initiation ceremony before they could become fishermen. This was known as 'brothering' and was performed in the presence of the crew of the boat they were to join, in a pub or loft. Hanging from the ceiling, through a block and tackle, was a noose which was fitted round the initiate's neck while he was forced to eat a salted roll. While he was choking down the roll, the skipper threw beer in his face and the mate drenched his legs with the same, each of them alternately repeated

the words 'weather' and 'lee' and the skipper pronouncing from time to time certain lines of fishing lore, such as:

'From St Abb's Head tae Flamborough Head,
Whane'er ye cut, be sure ye bend,
Ne'er lea a man wi' a loose end.'

Apparently, the beer in the face symbolised the spray of a 'weather' wave over the bow of the boat, while that over the legs signified water sweeping over the decks. The whole rite was looked upon as a sort of baptism and only after it had been done were they looked upon as grown men and treated as such by their shipmates.

Another curious custom attended the 'rapin' o' th' nets' (literally 'roping': fixing or mending). Before the nets were allowed to be used they had to be sprinkled with whisky and all the crew had to have a dram. If, during the 'rapin' ', a barefooted woman should step over the nets while they were spread out this was 'a blight to the hope of the nets' usefulness' and very unlucky. North of Eyemouth the coast continues in a sweep of crimson cliffs and sandy coves round Coldingham Bay, scene of many Viking landings in days gone by and now invaded annually by scuba-diving enthusiasts, drawn by the fact that the bay is a Marine Reserve. At the northwest end of the bay is the village of **St Abb's**, formerly called Coldingham Shore.

A harbour was not built at St Abbs until 1832 — prior to this date the boats were simply pulled up on the beach — and it was quickly realised that this provided an invaluable haven for boats fishing off the wild and rugged St Abbs Head. Another harbour, adjoining the original one,

EYEMOUTH FISHING DISASTER

The whole length of Great Britain's east coast suffered terrible destruction in the great gale of the 14th October 1881; the storm as ferocious on land as at sea.

For the fishing fleet of Eyemouth it was an experience never to be forgotten. Half the fishing fleet (23 boats) was sunk and 189 men drowned. Of this awesome total, 129 were Eyemouth fishermen. Of the remaining 60 fishermen, St Abb's lost three, Cove lost 11, Burnmouth lost 24, Newhaven lost 15 and Fisherrow lost 7 men. Scarcely a family in the town of Eyemouth did not suffer bereavement. Brothers went down with brothers, and fathers with sons.

The disaster hit Eyemouth when the town was going through a rising tide of prosperity. Eyemouth's fleet was second to none, with modern fishing craft and daring fishermen; it was crippled overnight.

Many lives have been lost and there was always tragedy, actual or threatened, connected with the fishing industry and this is expressed in this traditional local saying—

'Wha'll buy my caller herrin'?
They're no' brought here without brave darin'!
Buy my caller herrin'? Ye little ken their worth.

Wha'll buy my herrin'?
Oh, ye may ca' them vulgar farin',
Wives and mithers maist despairing
Ca' them lives o' men.'

Fast Castle

was constructed in 1890.

The fishing off St Abbs has been long esteemed — haddock, turbot and cod, the latter being pickled and sent to London; lobsters and crabs for the Edinburgh market; herrings in season, landed at Eyemouth for curing. Nowadays the only boats based in St Abbs are small lobster and crab boats, but the port is still much used by larger fishing boats in bad weather.

St Abbs itself is an attractive, tranquil place, with cottages along the harbour and randomly piled up the brae behind. On the harbour itself is a picturesque group of old 'net houses', used for storing fishing gear.

In days gone by it was customary to print the names of villagers lost at sea on small cards which were mounted on the walls of the fishers' cottages: a perpetual memorial and a continual reminder.

Between St Abbs and Cove, the next village up the coast, are the battered fragments of Fast Castle, once a great fortress belonging to the Home family. At one time Fast Castle was of considerable importance. Its position, with cliffs and sea on three sides and a moat and drawbridge on the fourth, made it virtually impregnable: in 1510 the Marshall of Berwick needed two thousand men to wrest it from its ten inhabitants.

By 1600 it was owned by Sir Robert Logan of Restalrig, one of the 'Gowrie Conspirators' who planned to kidnap King James VI and imprison him there. After the conspirators had been discovered and executed, Sir Robert was buried within the walls of his castle; nine years later his bones were dug up and tried for treason. There is a persistent legend that before he died he hid a hoard of treasure in Fast Castle.

The village of **Cove** stands on top of the headland opposite Cockburnspath. At the foot of the cliffs is a wide, rocky bay and, at first, no sign of a harbour or boat-strand. A steep footpath leads towards the sea and halfway down a tunnel has been hewn through the headland — popular in days gone by with smugglers. At the other end of the tunnel the sight that greets the visitor is breathtaking: one can agree with the writer of the New Statistical Account (1845) when he says, 'So perfectly secluded is this little bay and so unexpected is the scene which almost instantaneously opens to the view, that it produces on the mind of the stranger an almost electrical effect of surprise and admiration'.

The harbour was begun in 1770 but not finished until 1831. It is a rugged old pier with irregular steps, old mooring rings and bollards. On the pier-head are two dilapidated old fishermen's cottages, with creels and gear piled about them, used today as tackle-sheds, although the local council want to transform them into holiday homes.

The shore is a clean white beach and beyond it, with their backs to the steep hillside, are a couple of clean white cottages.

A century ago, haddock, cod, whiting, skate, halibut and herring were all landed here, and the village had its own cod-liver oil factory.

Today three or four small boats still fish for lobsters and crabs, and about half a dozen fishermen live in the village on the top of the brae.

Beyond Cove the county of East Lothian is entered; the coastline is gentler and is dominated by the unnaturally massive, ominous shape of

In certain Berwickshire villages, the minister, out of regard for the prejudices of the fisherfolk, will not go near the boats when the men are preparing to sail.

Torness power station as it continues in a north-westerly direction towards Dunbar. The only village on this stretch of coast is the tiny harbour of **Skateraw**, no longer used today, but once a welcome haven for boats running before an easterly wind and unable to make Dunbar.

Dunbar itself was once one of Scotland's most important ports and its history as a fishing village goes back many hundreds of years: in the sixteenth and seventeenth centuries, when large Dutch 'busses' (as well as local boats) unloaded their catches at the harbour, as many as 20,000 people converged on the town during the season. There were shipbuilders, sailmakers, rope workers and an iron foundry; in 1752 a whale fishery was established and carried on for over half a century; later there was a steam engine manufactory, a distillery and more than one brewery. Indeed the town was famous for its maltings, and is still the home of one of Scotland's most popular 'real' ales — 'Belhaven Beer'.

The first harbour built at Dunbar was known as 'The Old' or 'Cromwell' harbour and was constructed on the instructions, and with the financial support of the Lord Protector of England after he had defeated a royalist army outside the town in 1650. Many of the stones used in its creation were quarried from Dunbar Castle nearby, which was all but destroyed in the process.

'BLACK AGNES'

Dunbar Castle was an important fortress, and was often involved in the interminable wars between England and Scotland. The most celebrated occasion was in 1339 when the castle was held for five months against the forces of William de Montacute by the Countess of Dunbar and March. She was known as 'Black Agnes' because of an unusually swarthy complexion. The Earl of Dunbar was in the north; the defence of his stronghold left to his Countess.

During the siege, Agnes defied them, insulted them, killed every man who dared to come below the walls and generally performed all the duties of a skilled and courageous commander. When the English hurled boulders and lead balls against the battlements, she had one of the maidservants wipe away the dust thus caused with clean white napkins!

Ultimately, the English withdrew and this gallant act did much to preserve Scotland's independence.

The 'New' harbour immediately below the Old is also called 'The Victoria Harbour' and was built early in the reign of the great queen. Neither harbour is easy to enter except in still weather or light sou'west to west winds, which is somewhat surprising for a port that once hoped to rival

Dunbar

Peterhead and Fraserburgh as a whaling centre and was referred to as 'the Yarmouth of Scotland as regards red herrings'.

The port's decline in the 1920s was sudden and somewhat mysterious: local tradition maintained that it was because boats were permitted to fish on the Sabbath, and indeed the only other port of note that allowed this to happen was Stonehaven in Aberdeenshire, and Stonehaven suffered a similar decline.

In recent years, however, the fishing harbour at Dunbar has enjoyed a revival. Prawns, lobsters, crabs and some white fish are sought by a growing fleet of boats of varying sizes. At present there are about thirty commercial fishing boats working out of the port, more than there have been for sixty years, and to see them crowded into the tiny inner basin of the Old Harbour is a memorable sight.

The castellated battery between the Old and New harbours was used as a military hospital during the First World War.

The town itself has great charm. Built almost entirely of blood-red stone, it is full of wonderful old buildings in various stages of dilapidation and restoration.

The town of **North Berwick**, some fifteen miles from Dunbar, is almost as ancient as its neighbour, having received its Royal Charter from King Robert II in the fourteenth century. It was never such an important fishing centre, however, although during much of the last century there were more than 200 men sailing to the fishing from there. At one time the port even exported grain and potatoes. Today there are three or four small boats fishing for lobsters and

Port Seton

crabs from the harbour, and it is the base of the East Lothian Yacht Club.

BASS ROCK

A massive volcanic plug, rising sheer for 320 feet out of the Firth of Forth, the Bass Rock was a religious retreat in early times and then a prison for many centuries.

During the troubled reign of Robert III (1390-1406) — when it was said that 'there was no law in Scotland but he who was strong oppressed the weak and the whole kingdom was a den of thieves . . . and justice, outlawed, was in exile outwith the bounds of the kingdom' — the king's youngest son, James (later James I), was taken to the Bass Rock when he was eleven years old and trying to escape to France. He was there for a month, and when at last a ship bound for Danzig with a cargo of hides took him off it was captured by pirates and the unfortunate boy was handed over to the English king, Henry IV, who held him prisoner for 18 years.

The rock was purchased as a state prison in 1671. Charles II used it for the detention of presbyterian ministers, and later it was used to incarcerate Jacobites. In 1691 a group of Jacobite prisoners overpowered their guards and held the island for the King in Exile for three years, until they were starved into surrendering.

Today the population of the island consists of three lighthouse keepers and thousands of seabirds, mainly gannets, of which there are 30,000 breeding pairs.

Regular boat trips to the island run from North Berwick in the summer months.

Beyond North Berwick the coast continues low and sandy, with patches of wood and mudflats stretching out into the Forth at low tide. Then, at **Port Seton**, begins the ribbon of linked townships which stretch west to Leith — the harbour of Edinburgh — and beyond.

Port Seton and its close neighbour **Cockenzie** were both flourishing herring ports during the nineteenth century, the latter's harbour being opened in 1830 and the former's some fifty years later. Cockenzie harbour was built principally for shipping coal from the East Lothian collieries, and the town claims to have been the terminus of the oldest railway in the world — a line constructed on wooden blocks connecting the shore with Tranent coalfield and built in 1722.

It has been said — as it has been said of not a few fishing ports on the east coast — that 'there are no better seamen in Scotland than those from Cockenzie'. Certainly the fishing provided good livings for upwards of 700 souls in the two villages during the middle decades of the last century. In the winter there was a reliable trade in local oysters, and in cod, whiting and flounders caught in the Firth of Forth. In spring some of the men would travel to find berths in whaling ships from Leith or Peterhead, while others would take their own boats north to Caithness for the herring season. Port Seton has a fleet of seventeen prawn trawlers today, most of them using Eyemouth as a base during the season; there is no fishing from Cockenzie and the harbour is partially silted up, though there is a fine boat-building yard and a fish curer on the quayside.

Until the early 1950s Cockenzie and Seton fishermen held an annual procession through the villages, with singing and dancing, preceded by the ritual burning of an old boat on the foreshore to banish any bad luck that might have been encountered over the past year.

Nowadays both Seton, Cockenzie and the little village of **Prestonpans**, a mile up the coast, are

The Battle of Prestonpans

On the morning of 20th September 1745, Bonnie Prince Charlie's Highland army faced that of the Hanoverian government across a field of corn between Seton and Preston.

The Hanoverian commander, Sir John Cope, described them as 'a parcel of rabble; a parcel of brutes' as they approached, like a moving hedge, in absolute silence and at an incredible pace. When they were near enough they fired one volley, threw down their guns and raising a great scream, charged upon their foe.

The battle lasted ten minutes: for forty Highlanders, the government lost 400 men, with many more taken prisoner.

Musselburgh, once famous for its mussels, earned the title 'The Honest Toun' after the citizens turned down any reward for nursing the wounded Earl of Murray, Bruce's supporter who died in the town in 1322.

Mussel Brose

'At Musselburgh and eke' Newhaven
The fisher-wives will get top livin'
When lads gang oot on Sunday's even
To treat their joes
An' tak o' fat paudours a prieven
or mussel brose.'

Mussels, oatmeal, stock or milk-and-water

Wash the shells thoroughly, scraping them well, then put into a collander and rinse until the water runs clear of sand. Put aside and steep for two hours. Drain, and heat in a pan, covered by water, shaking until the shells open. Remove immediately. Strain the liquid and remove the mussels from the shells, discarding the beards and black parts. Bring the liquid and some fresh stock to the boil and add the mussels. Put a handful of toasted oatmeal in a bowl and dash a cupful of the mussel bree (stock) over it. Stir up quickly, return to the pan for a minute. Serve very hot.

dominated by the awe-inspiring bulk of Cockenzie power station.

Prestonpans takes its name from the extensive mediæval salt pans which were situated there. Run by monks, vast quantities of sea water were evaporated for the salt in it. In modern times, however, 240 acres of land have been reclaimed from what were once salt pans.

The village had its harbour at Morrison's Haven, and oysters were the main prize sought by the fishermen. In the 1760s the Firth of Forth yielded around 30 million oysters a year, and a single boat could dredge up 9,000 oysters a day to supply the numerous oyster shops and taverns of Edinburgh, with enough left over to send down 30 to 40,000 to Newcastle twice a season. Unusually, the fishermen of Prestonpans considered it lucky to put to sea on the Sabbath. There is no fishing from the village now, though it was the pollution of the Forth, and the resulting death of the oysters, that killed the trade, not the wrath of God — as at Dunbar and Stonehaven!

In spite of its name, **Musselburgh** has no harbour of its own and the fishing that was carried on from the town was all done from the formerly separate village of **Fisherrow**.

No commercial fishing boats use Fisherrow as a home port today, nevertheless there is still a strong community of fisher-folk, working out of other harbours, and each year a grand procession is held by them. The 'Fishermen's Walk' takes place on the first Friday in September—at the end of the old herring season. Those participating dress in the traditional garb —navy blue Guernseys for the men: striped petticoats and colourful shawls for the women. Led by bands and historic banners, and with a fisherman wearing the Fisherrow Medallion at its head, the procession winds through the streets of Fisherrow and Musselburgh and finishes up with sports and festivities in the grounds of Pinkie House.

The Fisherrow Medallion was given to the men of Fisherrow in 1796 for their role in defending Scotland against the threat of French invasion.

At Fisherrow the most taboo words among the fishing community were 'pig' and 'rat': they were referred to as 'curly tail' and 'lang tail'.

The fishwives of Fisherrow were almost as famous as those of Newhaven: '. . . a peculiar race, they did the work of men and had the manners of men, in addition to the strength of men. Their amusements too were masculine. They played golf long before it became the present-day fashionable sport of women. On Shrove Tuesday there was always a football match at Musselburgh between married and unmarried Fisherrow women, and it was the former who were nearly always victorious!'

Peter Anson, 1930

The **Port of Leith** is the harbour for Edinburgh, but was not absorbed by the Capital until the First World War and boasts a long and separate history.

The first mention of the place was in 1134 when King David I gave the fisheries of Leith to the Canongate canons, and in 1313 it is recorded that Edward II of England burned all the ships in the harbour. He returned the following year and set up camp there before the Battle of Bannockburn.

A village was not established there until 1329, when Robert the Bruce included Leith in his charter for Edinburgh, and during the Middle Ages trade was conducted with all Europe from there. By the eighteenth century Leith had become one of the chief depots in the country for the exportation of herring and cod, and fishing boats from ports as far away as Buckie would sail there with their dried and salted winter catches.

The principal ferry across the Forth also ran from there until the mid-nineteenth century. Known as 'Broad Ferry', as opposed to the 'Queen's Ferry' further west, two sloops, manned by four men each, sailed on every tide to Burntisland and Kinghorn, and later to Pettycur.

It was from Pettycur that Dr Thomas Guthrie, the famous preacher and philanthropist, sailed in 1815 to begin his studies at the University of Edinburgh (at the age of twelve — not an unusual age to start university in those days). It was a wet, blustery evening when he arrived at the ferry with his tutor, having walked the last ten miles to Pettycur because of the absence of public transport in Fife. The boatmen at first refused to take the boat out for only two passengers, but at last the ferry superintendent ordered them and they were joined by a woman passenger. They were no sooner out in the Firth than the crew tried to extort money out of the unfortunate boy and his tutor, saying that if they didn't pay twice the fare they would pitch them overboard. They were saved in the end by the third passenger, a fishwife, who silenced the crew with her sharp tongue and they arrived safely in Leith.

By the turn of the nineteenth century the docks had been expanded to handle an even greater volume of commercial shipping, and the fisher-

'I was down at Leith in the afternoon and, God bless me, what horrid women I saw; I never knew what a plain-looking race it was before. I was sick at heart with the looks of them. And the children, filthy and ragged. And the smells. And the fat black mud. . . . And yet the ships were beautiful to see as they are always; and on the pier there was a clean cold wind that smelt a little of the sea, though it came down the Firth, and the sunset had a certain éclat.'

Robert Louis Stevenson

Leith

men removed to Newhaven. The docks have been expanding ever since, and today they cover more than 600 acres in six large basins.

The fishing port for Edinburgh is **Newhaven**, 'Our Lady's Port of Grace' as it was originally named. The town was founded in 1488 by James III, who established a shipyard there which, 23 years later, built the biggest ship in the world.

The first fishing families to settle in Newhaven were Flemings who had come to Scotland to escape religious persecution, and until modern times much of the architecture in the older part of the town was in the Flemish style. In 1572 a Society of Free Fishermen was established along the lines of a Flemish guild.

Many old traditions lingered in Newhaven until modern times: for example, in the customs surrounding the weddings of the fisher-folk.

For some days before the marriage, the bride and bridesmaids would walk about the village dressed for the ceremony, inviting friends and relatives to the wedding. When the day came, a band of the groom's friends, wearing their best clothes — loose-fitting white trousers, velvet waistcoats and blue coats with brass buttons — would go to his house and march him under escort to the church. After the ceremony everybody would adjourn to the local hotel for a feast which would continue through the night until well into the afternoon of the following day.

coutouriers and became the fashion of the day. Their ordinary costume consisted of a white 'mutch' or handkerchief tied round their heads, a navy-blue bodice and skirt — the latter kilted up to show a blue and white striped petticoat, and the former with its sleeves tucked up as far as the elbow. Over her shoulders the woman would wear a blue serge cape to save her clothes from the dripping of the heavy creel, or basket, which hung from her shoulders.

> 'Wha'll buy my caller herrin'?
> They're bonnie fish and dainty farin'
> Wha'll buy my caller herrin'
> New drawn frae the Forth?'
> **Lady Nairn, 'Caller Herrin'**

They were renowned for their sharp tongues, which gave rise to the Scots expression 'a tongue life a fishwife', and until the 1950s they used to tramp into Edinburgh with their creels on their backs to sell fish from door to door, their cry of 'Caller Herrings' ('fresh herrings') echoing around the streets in the old town until it became a song. In its turn, the song was adopted by the City of Glasgow as a theme-song: until the middle of the nineteenth century Glasgow obtained all its herring from the Forth. Today there is still one fishwife who sells her fish from the pavement on Braid Road in Edinburgh three days a week, but she has a van now, rather than a creel.

Granton harbour, a mile west of Newhaven, was begun in 1837, 'with a broad approach road from the centre of Edinburgh'. It was financed by the Duke of Buccleuch and was intended to be the grandest port on the Forth and to be the principal ferry terminus for Fife and the north. It was opened on 28th June 1838, the day of Queen Victoria's coronation, and *The Times* correspondent remarked:

'I had repeatedly heard of this stupendous

During the Napoleonic Wars the Newhaven fishermen offered their services to the Royal Navy in great numbers. HMS *Texel*, 64-gun frigate, was manned entirely by Newhaven fishermen and after she captured a French ship-of-the-line the Free Fisherman's Society received a letter of congratulation from George III and a present of £250 from the City of Edinburgh.

Cabbie-Claw

'Cod-fish salted for a short time and not dried in the manner of common salt fish, and boiled with parsley and horse-radish. They eat it with egg-sauce, and it is very luscious and palatable.'
Capt. Topham, an English visitor to Edinburgh, 1774-5.

a codling, parsley, horse-radish, salt, pepper, water, egg-sauce

Take a fresh codling of about 3½ lbs. in weight; clean and skin it, and wipe it dry. Rub the fish inside and out with salt, and let it lie for twelve hours; then hang it up in the open air for twenty-four hours. Place in a saucepan with sufficient water to cover and bring to boil. Add three to four sprigs of parsley and a tablespoonful of grated horse-radish. Simmer very gently until the fish is cooked, but do not over-cook. Remove the fish, skin, lift all the flesh from the bone and divide neatly into small pieces. Arrange a border of hot mashed potato on a heated serving-dish, place the fish in the centre and cover with egg sauce. Serve very hot.

A Newhaven fishwife 'is always supposed to ask double or treble what she will take; and on occasions of bargaining, she is sure, in allusion to the hazardous nature of her gudeman's occupation, to tell her customers that the fish are 'no fish th' day, they're just men's lives'.
James Bertram, 1869

The Newhaven fishwives were famous throughout the country for their panâche and quick wits. During his visit to Edinburgh in 1822, George IV declared that they were the handsomest women he had ever seen, and sixty years later, when a group of eighteen fishwives attended an international fisheries exhibition in London, their costume so impressed visitors to the show that it was adopted by London

undertaking, its eligible situation, the facilities it afforded for the accommodation of passengers, goods, horses and carriages, embarking and disembarking, and the depth of water affording vessels at all times of the tide to approach it without danger. . . .'

Shortly after the opening, the Duke levied a toll of tuppence on every pedestrian using the new pier. Having just paid his due, a traveller who had been accosted by a beggar protested that he had given his last penny to the Duke of Buccleuch. 'What?' said the vagrant, 'is he upon the tramp too?'

The harbour quickly became an important fishing port and provided a home for a sizeable fleet of fishing boats until well into the twentieth century. Its heyday was just before the First World War when it rivalled even Aberdeen in importance, and as late as 1928 it had a fleet of 62 steam drifters. In the course of the same year 3,542 trawlers landed their catches at either Granton or Leith — some 459,874 cwt. of fish. Today the harbour is a mecca for yachtsmen and provides safe shelter for countless small boats. There is no commercial fishing done from there.

Cramond has never been a centre for fishing in spite of its very considerable antiquity. Situated at the mouth of the little River Almond, the harbour was of some importance in Roman times, and a camp was established there, at the eastern end of the Antonine Wall, to guard the harbour. It is likely that Septimus Severus' punitive expedition to the north of Scotland in A.D. 208 was mounted from there, and it is certain that the galleys which completed the first circumnavigation of the British Isles started out from Cramond.

The final fishing village in Lothian is **South Queensferry**, some six miles west of Cramond and really too far up the Forth to have harboured more than a handful of small boats at any time during its long history, although there was a profitable smuggling trade conducted between here and Fife.

The village was named after Queen Margaret, Malcolm Canmore's sainted consort in the eleventh century, and became famous for the ferries which crossed from there to North

Cramond Brig

Cramond Brig was built in 1619 and stands on the site of an earlier, wooden structure which was the scene of an attack on King James V (1513-42).

It was the King's custom to disguise himself as a commoner and to wander about his kingdom calling himself 'The Gudeman of Ballengeich'. An English spy of the time reported that this disguise fooled nobody and that as he passed by the true commonalty shouted 'there goes the King of Scots!'.

It seems, however, that it did deceive a band of gypsies at Cramond, for they attacked the King and would have robbed him had it not been for the intervention of the village miller, Jock Howieson. The miller attended the King's cuts and bruises, bringing him a towel and a basin of water, and in return the King granted him the lands of Braehead nearby, on condition that the Howieson heirs should be ready with a ewer of water and a basin to present to the Sovereign whenever he should pass.

To this day the obligation has continued to be fulfilled, and Howieson's descendants offered a basin and ewer to the present Queen in 1952 when she came by Cramond.

Queensferry, and thence to Dunfermline, where there was a holy shrine. A regular ferry was introduced by Queen Margaret's grandson, David I, and was originally run by the monks of

Dunfermline. There is an interesting 15th century Carmelite church in the village, associated with the pilgrim's path and well restored in 1890 as the episcopal parish church. It is the only medieval Carmelite church still in use in Britain. The old harbour of South Queensferry was built close under the churchyard wall and remains of it can still be seen there: from the early 18th century the harbour in front of the Hawes Inn — known formerly as the Hawes Harbour — was used by the ferries.

The Hawes Inn, an attractive eighteenth-century building, still operates as an hotel. It was the scene of David Balfour's kidnapping in Robert Louis Stevenson's famous novel *Kidnapped*.

Cove

William Collin,
drowned at sea, 1881.

FIFE

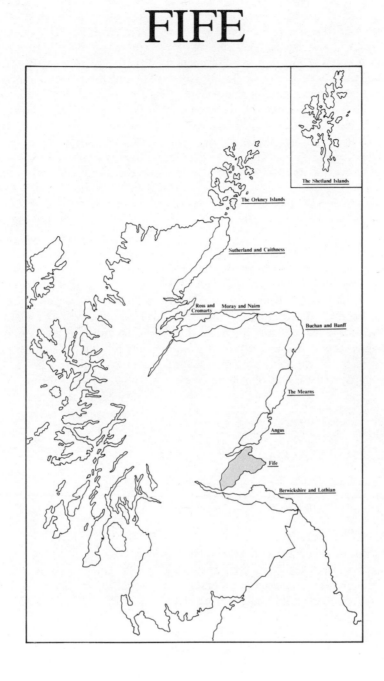

The Shetland Islands

The Orkney Islands

Sutherland and Caithness

Ross and Cromarty   Moray and Nairn

Buchan and Banff

The Mearns

Angus

Fife

Berwickshire and Lothian

When James VI (1542-1625) described his kingdom as having 'a fringe of gold' he was referring to the ancient ports of Fife, rather than the whole of the east coast of Scotland. Many of the north-eastern harbours had not even been built in King James' day, whereas the villages of the Firth of Forth plied an important and lucrative trade with the countries of Northern Europe, as well as being fishing centres.

Fife has long been proud of its independence and the peninsula has been known as 'The Kingdom of Fife' since time immemorial, probably because the ancient capital of Pictland, Abernethy, lies within its boundary. Even within the last ten years 'The Kingdom' successfully opposed the Government's regional reorganisation and avoided becoming part of Tayside Region.

Commercial fishing from the Fife villages has revived somewhat in recent years, with the large majority of the fleet being based at Pittenweem. The harbours along the coast may be divided into 'Forth Ports' and 'East Neuk'. The former are mainly industrial and are much changed from their hey-day as fishing centres: the latter have been restored rather than replaced and speak eloquently to the visitor of bygone ages....

> Oh blithely shines the bonnie sun upon the Isle of May,
> And blithely rolls the morning tide into St Andrews bay;
> When haddocks leave the Firth of Forth, and mussels leave the shore,
> When oysters climb up Berwick Law, we'll go to sea no more—
> No more—we'll go to sea no more.
>
> **Traditional**

THE FORTH PORTS

Although commercial fishing was carried out in several of the western harbours, the Forth Ports as I have termed them, it is now but a memory. In many of them, however, fishing never played a large part in local life: even in mediaeval times the principal maritime activity at **North Queensferry** was the ferrying of passengers across the Forth, and although there was a handful of boats fished from the little harbour, they were only ever after crabs and lobsters, and the occasional fish that strayed this far upstream.

The ferrymen themselves had a reputation for being surly and quarrelsome: in 1637 five of them were sent to gaol for refusing to carry the Lord of Doune across the river, and in the same decade the King himself (Charles I), having lost "Thirty-five of his servantes, his siller and hoosehold goodes" during a crossing, laid charges before the Privy Council, accusing the ferrymen of "practices that tended more to their own lucre than to our subjects good and saftie".

At **Inverkeithing**, as in many of the western Forth ports, the principal maritime activity was the exporting of coal.

The lasses o' the Ferry,
They busk braw;
The lasses o' the Elie,
They ding a';
The lasses o' St Monans,
They curse and ban;
The lasses o' Pittenweem-
They do the same;
The lasses o' Anster,
They drink strong yill;
There's green grass in Cellardyke
And crabs in till Crail.

Traditional

Today the wide harbour is dominated by a shipbreaker's yard and a paper mill. Industrial detritus litters the shore and the place has a scarred and melancholy air.

The town itself is not unlike its harbour, though there are some interesting 16th and 17th century buildings at its heart, including the birthplace of Admiral Sir Samuel Greig, the man who, in the mid-eighteenth century claimed to be the father of the Russian navy.

A short distance from the town is the desolate and recently demolished St David's harbour. In former times St David's sheltered a small fleet of fishing vessels and boasted a customs house. Now the little harbour is almost entirely silted up, but it is to be hoped that one day its picturesque setting might again be made use of.

Further downstream is another picturesque little harbour. **Aberdour**, formed by a narrow arm of headland protecting the mouth of the Dour burn, was once a thriving community of fishers. Today it is a popular seaside resort, with fine beaches in either direction and safe bathing.

Two miles off the pier lies the island of **Inchcolm**, the site of the famous, and very well-preserved, abbey, founded in 1173 by King Alexander I (1107-74) in gratitude to a hermit who came to his assistance when he was shipwrecked on the island.

Inchcolm

Tradition has it that **Burntisland** harbour was used by the Roman Emperor Agricola in 83 A.D., and there are the remains of a Roman fortification on Dunearn Hill behind the village. Certainly the harbour has long been in operation, and in the 16th and 17th centuries a thriving trade with the Baltic and the Low Countries was conducted from there: in the 19th century the main export was coal, indeed more coal passed through Burntisland than any other port in Fife. The harbour was also the terminus of the Firth of Forth Rail Ferry, the first rail ferry in the world. At the same time it was an important fishing port, particularly known for the curing of fish. During the middle decades of the last century there were as many as 500 boats landing

urntisland for salted
herring,
inghorn for cursing
and swearing.'
Traditional

fish at Burntisland during the season, while a small fleet of ships sailed north to the Caithness herring run in the summer, loaded with barrels and salt in order to bring back cured fish.

The village has a fine church, built in 1592, with an anchor carved over its door. Here, in 1601, the General Assembly of the Church of Scotland met in the presence of King James VI—there being an outbreak of plague in Edinburgh—and discussed for the first time the proposal that the Bible be translated into English.

Today the port is used mainly for the importing of bauxite from Brazil and for the exporting of alumina to Scandinavia. The cranes and sheds of the Burntisland Shipbuilding Company loom over the inner harbour, though the yard is now closed and there is little sign of the fishing industry that once thrived there.

There is even less sign of fishing in the quaint little cove of **Pettycur**, which was silted up over 50 years ago.

The fact that Pettycur appears on all the old milestones in Fife might lead one to suppose that it had once been a substantial community—the Kirkcaldy or Leven of its day. The fact is that the principal ferry across the Forth east of Queensferry ran from here and was used by the Royal Mail coaches travelling north and south. The harbour was also a famous spot for smuggling. Above the harbour, close to **Kinghorn** village, is a high mound, known locally as the 'Crying Hill'. It is likely that watchers from here spied out the great shoals of herring coming up the Forth and called the news down to the waiting fishermen below.

Kinghorn itself once had a number of celebrated shipyards and a sizeable fishing fleet, much depleted even a hundred years ago. There is a fine old church on the very edge of the shore, in which sailors had a chartered right to use the south aisle, both during services and at other times. It was customary for the fishermen to hold their meetings there, and in wet weather the place was used as a social club.

Just south of the town a monument marks the spot where King Alexander III met his death by falling from his horse in 1286.

Two and a half miles out into the Forth lies the island of **Inchkeith**, associated with a curious experiment conducted by James IV (1488-1513). The King was a keen 'scientist' and, in order to investigate what man's original speech might have been, incarcerated two infants on the island, under the protection of a dumb nurse. Popular thought of the day reckoned they would speak either Hebrew or Gaelic; in fact they could speak not a word.

Kirkcaldy is known as 'the lang toun' and was described by Daniel Defoe in the seventeenth century as being 'one street a mile long': today this street is 4 miles long.

It has been an important port for several centuries, and in 1779, during the American War of Independence, the American naval hero John Paul Jones anchored off the town and threatened to shell it unless he was paid £200,000. The day was saved by a local priest, who successfully prayed on the beach for a strong off-shore wind to drive the raiders out to sea.

Kirkcaldy harbour was only built in 1840, though there had been an earlier and more primitive port there prior to this date. The 'new' harbour was not built for the fishing but for the whaling, which was an important industry in Kirkcaldy at the time. A large blubber works was also built behind the pier.

Kirkcaldy has three famous sons: Michael Scott (b. 1175), one of the most learned men of his day, who became Professor of Rhetoric at the University of Bologna and is known to popular history as a magician; Adam Smith (b. 1723), the author of 'The Wealth of Nations'—a book that was in fact written in Kirkcaldy after his travels in the United States; and Robert Adam (b. 1728), Scotland's greatest architect.

On the eastern end of Kirkcaldy, and part of the larger town, is the pretty little harbour of **Dysart**, an independent burgh until 1928, known as the 'saut burgh' after the extensive salt pans nearby, and today preserved by the National Trust.

Salt, along with beer, coal and cured fish, was exported from Dysart to Holland in return for 'cart wheels and delft-ware, kegs of Hollands and pipes of Rhenish' in such quantities that the village became known as 'Little Holland'. It was the birthplace of John MacDouall Stuart, the explorer of Central Australia.

In 1700 Daniel Defoe described **Buckhaven** as 'a miserable Row of Cottage-like Buildings' and today, surrounded by the large town of Methil, it

ysart they call't; its
black and sulphurous
caves,
elch smoke and bellow
o'er the neighbouring
waves.
George Buchanan

ysart for coal and saut,
athhead for meal and
maut,
irkcaldy for lasses
braw,
inghorn for breaking
the law.
Traditional

Largo today, although there were 36 herring boats based there in 1855, employing 80 men and boys.

Buckhaven

still looks rather unprepossessing. The harbour has been filled in and grassed over.

It is said that the founders of Buckhaven were Dutch — from a ship that was wrecked on this part of the coast in about 1500 — and from earliest times fishing was the principal occupation of the inhabitants. Defoe went on to say that the populace were 'employed wholly in catching fresh fish every day in the Firth, and carrying them to Leith and Edinburgh markets. (So successful were they that, in spite of their poor cottages) . . . there is scarcely a poor man in it; but they are in general so very clownish that to be of the village of Buckhaven is become a proverb.' Right up to modern times, when fishing was replaced by the exporting of coal, Buckhaven men had a confident manner and a reputation for steadiness and reliability.

Nowadays the port of **Methil** has taken over from Buckhaven and serves both the latter village and the sizeable holiday resort of **Leven**. Methil docks are still used commercially, though not for fishing, and during both World Wars formed an important convoy centre. One of Leven's famous sons was Sir Alexander Gibson, a High Court judge of the seventeenth century who was kidnapped near his home by a masked gang of thugs, hired by defendants in a case he was shortly to try. Once the case had been heard by another judge, Sir Alex was returned safely to his family.

Beyond Leven the industrial West of Fife is left behind and **Largo** village is the first that has the appearance of a true fishing harbour. In fact, little or no commercial fishing is pursued from

ROBINSON CRUSOE

Alexander Selkirk, the model for Daniel Defoe's 'Robinson Crusoe', was born at Lower Largo in 1676. Although at an early age he voiced a desire to pursue the seafaring life, he was brought up in his father's trade of shoemaking and it took a violent family row and a solemn rebuke in church to finally persuade his family to let him leave home for the sea.

Once started on his new career, Selkirk proved himself an able seaman, finishing up as sailing master on the ageing and overcrowded brigantine *Cinque Ports*. An unhappy ship, there was continual quarrelling between the captain and his crew, and particularly with the sailing master, who regarded the ship as hardly seaworthy.

Selkirk resolved to leave the vessel as soon as it reached land, and when the ship anchored off the volcanic islands of Juan Fernandez, he decided to take his chance on Mas a Tierra. The captain was delighted, and Selkirk's shipmates rowed him and some supplies ashore and left him on the desolate beach. Even a desert island was preferable to the *Cinque Ports* and, in fact, the ship sank soon after he left it.

He slowly grew reconciled to his plight and set to work exploring the island and making a home for himself. Wild goats, sea-lions, turtles, shellfish and an abundance of fruit provided him with a healthy diet, and he restored a tiny hut which had been built by the original discoverers of the island.

Four years and four months passed by, and then an Englishman, Captain Woodes Rogers, who was on a privateering cruise, found Selkirk and brought him back to England.

Daniel Defoe expressed an interest in the case and Captain Rogers arranged a meeting with the castaway. 'Robinson Crusoe' appeared six years later and was an immediate bestseller. Selkirk died of yellow fever the following year aboard the *Weymouth*, aged only forty-four.

THE EAST NEUK

At **Earlsferry**, the western end of the village of Elie, the East Neuk of Fife is entered.

Earlsferry is described as 'old beyond the memory of man' in its sixteenth century charter, and it was from here that MacDuff, Earl and 'Thane' of Fife, fled from King MacBeth (1040-57) to Dunbar. Local fishermen helped him escape after first hiding him in a cave on Kincraig Point, known ever after as MacDuff's Cave, and between this point and Fife Ness arcs a fine sandy beach upon which garnets may be found.

Elie harbour itself was built in the sixteenth century, at which time it was the most important port on the Fife coast, conducting an extensive trade with Europe. The harbour itself has not been used for commercial fishing for many years and today it provides a haven for the many dinghies and small craft owned by visitors and locals alike.

To the east of the harbour stands the ruined Lady's Tower, named after Lady Janet Anstruther, a noted local beauty who used to bathe from it — having first sent a bell-ringer through the streets to warn people to keep away. St Monan was a Celtic missionary and the village of **St Monans**, or St Monance, grew up around a spring which was dedicated to the saint.

King David II, Robert the Bruce's son, founded a church in the village in 1362 in gratitude for his recovery from a wound at the saint's shrine, and until modern times the fishers of St Monans used to wash their nets and lines in the spring — not for luck, but because the water there had so much iron in it that it made the nets more durable.

The village motto is 'We live by the Sea', and when the wind is in the south east, sea spray blows over the fishers' graves in the old cemetery by the church. For centuries fishermen have been buried there, and for centuries St Monans was an important harbour: during the summer season the kirk bell was stopped from ringing, as the fishermen believed it frightened the fish out to sea.

'A minister came to preach on Sunday in this old church and chose for his text the parable of the prodigal son. He was not aware that in fishing circles the words "pig" or "swine" are taboo. Hence his astonishment was extreme on reading the words "and he sent him into the fields to feed swine", a simultaneous mutter of "Touch cauld iron",* accompanied by a general bowing down towards cuddy heels and heads of nails in the pews, took place. After a dismayed pause, the minister concluded that this was the people's way of saying "Amen", so he resumed the next sentence — "to feed swine". Again the whisper of "cauld iron", again the universal bowing of heads, again the minister's amazement, but mixed with a little indignation now. For the third time he spoke the fatal word, "the husks that the swine did eat", but, unable to stand this third awful shock, the congregation rushed helter-skelter from the church with a parting yell of "Touch cauld iron".'

'From the Forth Bridge to the East Neuk of Fife'
Jessie Patrick Findlay

1766 an Earlsferry
oat capsized in a gale.
ut of only eighteen
cal fishermen, six
ere lost.

St Monans

*Touching metal was supposed to ward off bad luck, in the same way as we might say, 'Touch wood'.

Close to the harbour is one of the oldest surviving boatbuilders in Scotland — Miller's Yard: established in 1747 and still building fishing boats with the time-won skills of master craftsmen.

On the 19th November 1875 five Fifeshire boats were lost while returning home from Northumbrian waters. Fifteen Cellardyke men, twenty-one St Monans men including the husband, son, two brothers, brother-in-law and cousin of a certain Mrs Paterson, were all drowned; some of the worst losses being at the harbour mouth.

In 1765, on the 15th of May at the shore of Pittenweem, a haddock fishing boat and the eight men aboard were lost. The widows and orphans were sent fifteen guineas by way of a Christian gift from Sir Harry Erskine.

It is supposed that **Pittenweem** derives its name from 'pit' a hollow and 'weem' a cave, and certainly there is a cave in the village named after St Fillan, which was originally a monastic shrine and which was later used by the fishermen for storing their gear. It has now been restored to its former purpose, and from time to time services are held there.

In 1705 one Janet Cornfoot was done to death in Pittenweem as a witch, after a series of wild accusations originating from an epileptic youth. The poor woman was first tortured by the minister and then dragged through the town and stoned to death in the presence of the magistrates.

Thirty years later a robbery occurred in the village which led to the famous Porteous Riots in Edinburgh. Two local fishermen robbed a customs officer, were caught and hanged in the Capital, and the Edinburgh mob rampaged through the streets in their support, and against the excise duties. Captain Porteous, the commander of the City Guard, was sent out to quell the riot and was lynched for his pains.

There has been a harbour at Pittenweem for centuries, and it was mainly used for trading with the Low Countries and the Baltic. The present pier and wharf were built in 1830. Unlike many of the other Fife ports, fishing at Pittenweem has gained in importance in modern times. At the height of the herring boom, in the 1890s, most of the boats sailed from Anstruther and St Monans, but today Pittenweem has taken over as the home port of the East Neuk fleet and there is a thriving fish market to handle the catches.

Until the Second World War, when the herring mysteriously abandoned the Firth of Forth, **Anstruther**, with its main harbour at adjoining **Cellardyke**, was the principal port in Fife. Indeed, it was one of the main ports in the east of Scotland, having a fleet of 221 boats in 1881 and employing nearly 600 fishermen.

The boats sailed south to Lowestoft in the autumn in time for the English herring season, and north to Lewis in the early spring for the west coast fishing, and in between times they sold their catches to the many curers who plied their trade at Anstruther.

Anstruther

Pittenweem

ne Miss Reid of
ellardyke (d. 1873)
st two husbands, two
ns, two sons-in-law,
o brothers and three
others-in-law during
r lifetime, all to the
a.

e old harbour of
ellardyke was the
ene of two of the
ddest fishing
agedies on the Fife
ast. On the 23rd
ptember 1793, seven
en died and one
rvived, within view of
latives, and also by
extraordinary
incidence in February
1800 seven men
ain were lost, with
e survivor.

/hen Paul Jones' fleet
pproached Cellardyke
1778 and signalled
r a pilot, the
shermen, suspicious,
sregarded his
mmons. A cannon-
ll whizzed over their
eads and was seen to
lash into a boggy
arsh. When the public
hool was being built
that site in the late
neteenth century the
asons found a rusty
nnonball—no doubt
e very one fired by
aul Jones.

Barrels of herring were sent to Russia, Scandinavia and the Baltic countries: smoked haddocks and pickled cod to Glasgow, Liverpool and London. The curers, or 'cadgers' as they were called, were a rough crew: 'a set of loud-mouthed fellows . . . their big blue bonnets pulled belligerently down to the nape of their necks — ready for anything, from selling a herring to engaging in single combat with a customer who was inclined to haggle a little about the price'.

There is no curing done in Anstruther nowadays, and the boats based in the harbour are mainly small, fishing lobsters, crabs and scampi.

> In the 'Memorials of Cellardyke' there is an interesting description of a typical fisherman's cottage of about 1800: The house had one tiny room, with an earth floor, unplastered walls and rough-hewn roof timbers. The open fireplace filled the whole room with smoke and beside it stood a low stool, the only seat in the place. Such light as penetrated the cloth curtain came from a small window glazed with coarse greenish glass, under which sat a sea chest containing the family's clothes. In a dark recess, known as 'the close', was a double box bed, and the only other furniture was a wooden cupboard (the 'press'), a table and a corner shelf holding a few dishes and ornaments brought back from voyages.

Many 'Anster-folk' have dark complexions, and tradition attributes this to a number of Spanish sailors who settled in the neighbourhood after the Armada in 1588. 260 Spaniards who had lost their ship suddenly arrived at the harbour,

armed to the teeth and destitute. The kindly folk of Anstruther, who had no quarrel with the King of Spain, took them in hospitably and helped those who wanted to return to their own country: many settled in the town however. The Spanish leader, Jan Gomez de Midini, later became an admiral and he never forgot the kindness of the people of Anstruther. Years later he secured the release of a Fife ship which had been captured by the Spanish navy, entertaining the crew at his own table.

The Scottish Fisheries Museum

Until the herring left the Forth in the 1940s, Anstruther was one of the principal ports on the east coast, so it is appropriate that the town be the site of Scotland's leading fisheries museum.

The museum is housed in one of the oldest identifiable property sites in any Scottish town, a group of buildings known as St Ayles Land, with a charter dated 1318. It holds a wide range of exhibits, historical and contemporary — from a trinket box fashioned out of a mussel shell to a modern wheelhouse, with such features as an aquarium, a whaling exhibition, old and new fishing equipment, fishermen's personal belongings, models of fishing boats and fisherfolk, maps of fishing grounds and information about related industries such as sailmaking and boatbuilding.

The easter-most of the Fife harbours is **Crail**, once one of the most important centres of Scotland's trade with Europe, and still retaining the appearance of a sixteenth century township. As far back as the ninth century Crail was

Crail

exporting salt fish to the Continent, and it is said that the Dutch learned the art of curing fish here. A local delicacy is the 'Crail Capon': a haddock smoked in the chimney lum.

In the early eighteenth century Crail was an important resort for herring fishermen from Aberdeen, Angus and the Mearns and immense quantities of fish were cured for home consumption. An 'Admiral Deputy' was appointed by the Crown to 'Try all Offenses relating to Fishing and to Fine or Otherwise Punish them'. He had his own boat to keep an eye on the fishing boats, and one of his duties was to fire a gun announcing the beginning and end of the week's fishing.

Curiously, the men of Crail were permitted to fish on Sundays by an ancient charter from Robert the Bruce, and it was this fact that caused

STATISTICS FROM 1881

	Number of Boats	Resident Fishermen
Aberdour	5	8
Kinghorn	11	20
Kirkcaldy	18	27
Dysart	6	10
Buckhaven	198	410
Leven	1	3
Largo	34	60
Elie/Earlsferry	13	24
St Monans	147	405
Pittenweem	91	240
Anstruther/Cellardyke	221	573
Crail	34	50

Compiled from the official reports of the Scottish Fishery Board 1881. (See below.)

In 1928 and 1977 the numbers were as follows:

Aberdour	1 boat	Largo	10 boats
Kinghorn	12 boats	St Monans	65 boats (1977: 13 boats)
Kirkcaldy	39 boats (1977: 1 boat)	Pittenweem	41 boats (1977: 31 boats)
Dysart	23 boats	Anstruther/	
Buckhaven	17 boats	Cellardyke	63 boats (1977: 37 boats)
Leven	3 boats (1977: 8 boats)	Crail	19 boats (1977: 9 boats)

St Andrews

John Knox to preach one of his most violent sermons in the parish kirk above the harbour.

Outside the church is a stone which is reputed to have been hurled at the village by the Devil when he visited the Isle of May, six miles away, and inside is another, the Crail Cross, an eighth century Pictish slab.

Between Crail and Fife Ness is the cave in which King Constantine, the son of Kenneth MacAlpin, was beheaded by the Danes in 877.

Legend has it that St Regulus, or St Rule as he is known, was shipwrecked off the north coast of Fife in the fourth century, bearing the relics of the apostolic fisherman St Andrew. The religious settlement founded on the spot became the greatest ecclesiastical centre in Scotland, **St Andrews.**

During the fifteenth and sixteenth centuries St Andrews was one of the most important seaports north of the Forth and conducted a thriving trade with all the trading ports of northern Europe: it is said that there were usually between two and three hundred vessels in the harbour during the great April festival, the Senzie Market, held until the Reformation.

After the Reformation trade fell off, and in 1656 one of Cromwell's Commissioners of Customs described the town as 'a pretty neat thing which hath formerly been bigger, and although sufficiently humbled in the time of the intestine troubles, continues still proud in the ruines of

her former magnificence'. At that time there were only three boats in the harbour.

In 1728 it was reported that St Andrews Bay 'abounds not only in cod and other white fish, but in herring also in their season', but that because the fishermen could only afford to use small boats they were 'half starved for want of business; and were the inhabitants able to fit busses [larger craft with covered decks] they could not be anywhere better served'. Fifty years later a storm carried away three out of the five small boats fishing from St Andrews.

St Andrews University is the oldest in Scotland, and the second oldest in Britain. It was founded by Papal Bull in 1413, and abounds with ancient traditions, one of which is 'pier walking'.

St Andrews undergraduates wear scarlet academic gowns (it is said that scarlet was chosen as the colour so that the students could be spotted as they went into the brothels: students of divinity wear black gowns — they are above suspicion!) and at certain times, particularly after chapel on Sunday morning, it is customary for them to progress down the pier wearing their gowns. This custom originated in the days when preachers at the university chapel arrived by sea, and it was deemed courteous to see them away safely.

The harbour is formed around a small natural creek at the mouth of the Kinness Burn and has a 420-foot long pier acting as a breakwater to its entrance. There is both an inner and an outer harbour, but both dry out at low water and even at high water there is not sufficient water to

Fife Fishing Families

Buckhaven: Logie, Robinson, Thomson.
St Monans: Aitken, Gowans, Marr, Reekie, Scott, Smith, Wood.
Anstruther and Cellardyke: Cunningham, Gardiner, Muir, Rodger, Watson.

admit boats of any size.

Because of this, St Andrews was never so important a fishing port as the East Neuk harbours, further south, nevertheless there were 14 vessels based there in 1838, and during the herring boom it was a home for 56 boats. Today the harbour shelters a couple of lobster boats and a flotilla of yachts and private craft.

Local sayings:

'**Speirin' the road to Crail'**—asking a question when you already know the answer.

'**Takin' saut tae Dysart'**—doing something unnecessary (as 'carrying coals to Newcastle').

'**Here come the Dykers, tenpence the score'**—'Dykers' were folk from Cellardyke, who had a reputation for parsimony and who put little into the collection plates, except in their home kirk.

'**Like a coo roarin' aff the Mey'**—a reprimand to someone talking loudly: the Island of May lies five miles off Crail.

'I have visited most of the Scottish fishing villages and many of the English ones, nor have I neglected Normandy, Brittany and Picardy; and wherever I went I found the fisherfolk to be the same, no matter where they talked a French patois or a Scottish dialect. . . . The manners, customs, mode of life, even the dress and superstitions, are nearly the same on the coast of France as they are on the coast of Fife.'

James Bertram, 1869

Partan Bree *(Crab Soup)*

Crabs, rice, white stock, salt, pepper, anchovy, cream.

Pick all the meat from two cooked crabs and set aside from the claw meat. Boil five or six ounces of rice in milk till soft and pass through a sieve with the crab meat into a basin. Stir it with a wooden spoon till perfectly smooth and add, very gradually, sufficient white stock for a party of twelve or fourteen people. Do not make it as thick as a puree. Season with salt, white pepper and anchovy. Put it all into a pan and stir it over a low heat. Do not boil. Add pieces of meat from the claws and, just before serving, stir in half a pint of cream.

Partan Pie

Partan (crab), salt, white pepper, nutmeg, butter, bread, vinegar, mustard (optional).

Having cooked the crab, pick the meat out of the claws and body; add to this a few knobs of fresh butter and some breadcrumbs. Season with salt, white pepper and nutmeg. Shake up a mixture of wine vinegar, olive oil and French mustard, and add this to the mixture. Cover with breadcrumbs and, having placed two or three knobs of butter on top, brown under the grill.

A wee drappy dram that's well sweetened and nappy,
With a pipe o' tobacco to pass the time happy;
A reeking hot pye, and a bicker o' ale,
And weel-butter'd haddocks ca'd capons o' Crail;
In rich ingan sauce, Scotch collops weel fried;
Gude beef and greens, wi' mustard supplied;
Partans, and lobsters, and whitings a score,
Invite to the fireside o' good Mary More.
Then helter-skelter the punch flies around,
And such other liquors as here may be found:
Deel care though they a' should fill themselves fou,
It's aften the case, and naething that's new.

'A Macaronic' by Tom Dishington, Late Clerk of Crail (1824)

ANGUS

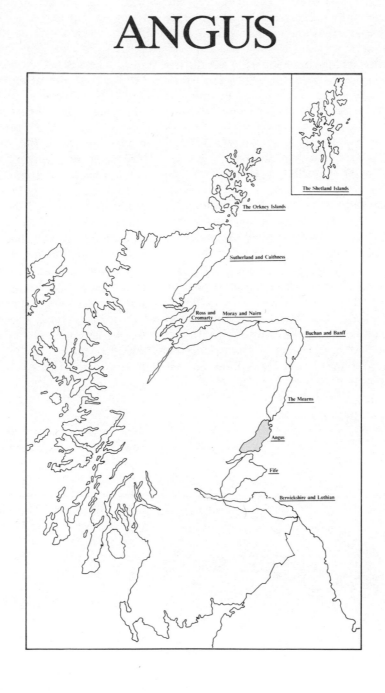

The Shetland Islands

The Orkney Islands

Sutherland and Caithness

Ross and
Cromarty   Moray and Nairn

Buchan and Banff

The Mearns

Angus

Fife

Berwickshire and Lothian

The Angus coast runs from the Firth of Tay to Montrose Bay. To the south it is low and undulating; further north it becomes steep and rugged; along its whole length it is exposed to the prevailing east winds and has few good natural harbours.

Most of the fishing communities in the district grew up around tiny coves with small, stony beaches, where the boats could be dragged ashore. They fished mainly for white fish (cod, haddock, ling) or shell fish (mussels, oysters, lobsters, crabs) close in to the shore; several of the villages became salmon stations.

Until the middle of the 18th century there was no herring fishery in the area, for this required larger, decked boats capable of sailing far further offshore than the small boats available. Except for a few harbours, the Angus coves simply couldn't accommodate such craft.

Another factor influencing the use of larger boats was cost. Even at **Dundee**, well sheltered in the Firth of Tay, it was remarked in 1770 that: "There are only three small fishing boats at this place, and what they take is insufficient for the towns on the coast, and they use no lines for great cod and ling. About Mar's Bank and the Cape, they say there are a great plenty of these fish; but they would required decked sloops to do things to purpose there." *(John Knox)*

As early as the 12th century the town had become an important trading port, and by the 18th century docks and wharfs had been built along the Tay to the east of the fishing harbour. By this time the town had grown into one of Scotland's principal manufacturing centres, with linen and textiles as the leading industries (at one time almost all the canvas sails for the Royal Navy were made at Dundee) and with more than one successful shipyard. Between 1871 and 1881, 2,075 ships were built there, of an average weight of 400 tons.

Yet the fishing, which had never been a major trade in the town, declined to such an extent that the writer of the 'New Statistical Account' (1845) could say 'the other fishings of Dundee are of no value'.

The only form of fishing which was 'of value' was whaling. Dundee had carried on a thriving whale and seal industry since the 18th century (both were regarded as 'fishings') and by the mid-19th century was sending a dozen screw-driven ships north in search of the great sea beasts, becoming second only to Peterhead as a whaling centre.

Every whaling ship carried between six and eight boats, each equipped with a harpoon gun mounted on its bows. As soon as a whale was sighted the boats were lowered with a crew of six men to give chase, and when they were close enough the harpoon was fired. The harpoon used in the Arctic was not sufficiently powerful to kill the whale and was merely a means of attaching the boat to the massive mammal until it tired sufficiently for the harpooner to either plunge a long shafted spear into its heart or fire an exploding dart into its body. Sometimes the plunging, stricken beast would tow the boat for several miles.

After death the carcass was towed back to the mother ship and the blubber was removed from it in a long spiral strip — the whale's body being revolved in the water alongside the ship to achieve this — then the blubber was cut into smaller pieces, stowed in barrels and taken back home. The raw carcass of the great creature was abandoned to the sea.

The last whaler at Dundee was the *Terra Nova*, launched in 1884. Whaling continued from the port for twenty years after this, with rising prices supporting the small catches, but by this time whales had disappeared from whole tracts of the Arctic, and the whalers were concentrating on the Southern Ocean. At the outbreak of the First World War all the whalers in Dundee which were still afloat were commandeered by the Royal Navy and sunk while carrying munitions to Russia.

At one time an attempt was made to emulate Aberdeen as a fish distribution centre, and although a successful fish market was

With the coming of steam-powered whalers in 1856, Dundee became the premier whaling port in the British Isles.

Dundee

'By its public buildings, by its latest extensions, its crowded harbour, by its great and numerous factories, by its exhibitions of enterprise and opulence, and by, here and there, a dash of the picturesque, Dundee offers large compensation for what it wants in the neat forms and elegant attractions of simple beauty.'
Ordnance Gazetteer of Scotland, 1884

It is likely that the first settlement at Dundee was a community of fisher-folk, and the prevalence of Pictish symbol stones and Celtic cross slabs in the vicinity indicates that there was an important settlement here at a very early date. The township grew up between St Nicholas Craig (now Craig Pier, close to the new swimming baths) and Castlehill Promontory, where the Tay Road Bridge enters the city. These two rocky headlands created a sheltered bay and in time this became the fishing harbour. It has since been filled in and the only sign of it today is the old beacon which used to guide the boats into the harbour-mouth, rising like a little light-house from the lawns and rose-beds of a small park close to the bridge.

established, with fishwives carrying in creels of fish every day from villages like Auchmithie, 24 miles away, it was never on the scale of the northern town.

> Whalers normally left Dundee in April, the departure coinciding with a local holiday. They would not return for at least six months, and there was the considerable risk of their not returning at all.
>
> Ships were frequently trapped by ice throughout the Arctic winter, with near starvation and scurvy amongst the crew as a result. Sometimes ships were crushed by the shifting tons of ice: in 1837 both the *Thomas* and the *Advice* were crushed by ice. The *Advice* remained afloat, though only just, and was found months later with only seven of her 49 crew remaining alive.
>
> So it is hardly surprising that the send-off given to boats about to depart for the frozen north was often so tremendous that the ships had to heave-to at the mouth of the Tay until the crews were sober enough to negotiate the narrow channel into the open sea.

Indeed it was said that the City of Dundee itself was supplied with white fish by the little village of **Broughty Ferry**, three miles to the east.

The history of Broughty Ferry is really that of its castle, an important stronghold controlling the mouth of the Tay and at times ranked as a fortress of national significance. The present castle was built by Lord Gray in 1498 and stands dramatically on Broughty Craig, thrusting out into the Firth of Tay. Today it is a museum and has an interesting collection of fishing and whaling relics, as well as a fine lifeboat display

'Bruchtie' or 'Brochite' means 'The Porch of Tay'.

> **Angus Fish Soup**
>
> 6 fresh haddocks' heads
> 2 pints water
> 1 small carrot
> 1 slice turnip
> 1 stick celery
> 3-4 sprigs parsley
> salt and pepper
> 2 oz butter
> 2 oz flour
> ½ pint milk
> 1 egg yolk
> 1 tb. sp. double cream
>
> Rinse the heads of the haddocks and place in a pan with the cold water. Bring to the boil and skim well, then add the vegetables, parsley and seasoning. Simmer until the vegetables are tender then strain, pressing the soft vegetables through the sieve.
>
> Melt the butter in the cleaned pan; add flour and make a white roux. Gradually add the strained broth and then the milk. Cook for a few minutes, adjust the seasoning, blend in the egg yolk and cream, and heat the whole through without boiling. Serve immediately, garnished with chopped parsley.

Mary Wollstonecroft, the author of *Franken-stein*, lived in a cottage near Peep o' Day Lane in Dundee. She eloped from there with Percy Bysshe Shelley, the poet.

and many local curiosities.

Tucked in beneath the massive square tower is the little harbour, formed by an L-shaped pier which was built in 1872, at the height of Broughty Ferry's prosperity. At this time 100 'fully decked boats' were based there during the summer months, though not all of them were manned by local fishermen. Then, only ten years after the completion of the harbour, the steam trawler arrived. The harbour was not big enough to accommodate the larger boats, and at the same time the price of fish dropped as the market was flooded by the quantities taken in deep water.

The line fishermen of Broughty hung on grimly (there were still 50 boats there in 1900: 12 in the 1920s) but its day as a fishing port was done.

About the same time as the arrival of the steam drifter, the attractions of fresh air and sea bathing drew many of Dundee's industrial barons to Broughty Ferry. A number of huge mansions were built in the vicinity of the town, and in the 1890s it was said that more wealth was concentrated here than in any other area of comparable size in the whole country.

Today the town has almost been absorbed by Dundee, yet in spite of its popularity as a residential suburb and a seaside resort, Broughty Ferry still retains an independent identity from its sprawling neighbour, an independence which is physically demonstrated by the cluster of old fishermen's cottages along the sea-front, so different from any buildings to be found in Dundee.

> **The Lifeboats at Broughty Ferry**
>
> There has been a lifeboat at Broughty Ferry since 1838, the earliest ones being manned by five local fishermen who were paid 10/- each for every life saved.
>
> The most famous lifeboat based there was the *Mona*, launched in 1935 and responsible for saving 118 lives. On Tuesday, 8th December 1959, the *Mona* was launched to assist the North Carr lightship, which had broken adrift. Her last radio message was received at 4.48 a.m., and after a helicopter search the stricken lifeboat was found on Buddon Sands: she had capsized in the terrific sea and her crew of eight were all drowned. Today a large 'Avon' class lifeboat, the *Spirit of Tay*, is moored off the old lifeboat shed. Like her predecessors, she was bought by public subscription. She cost £250,000 and was launched in 1978.

East of Broughty Ferry the shoreline continues low and sandy past Monifieth and round Buddon Ness to Carnoustie.

The area has been inhabited by man since the dawn of time and many relics and sites of archaeological interest stand witness to this. Several Pictish symbol stones were found at Monifieth, for example, and are now held in the Museum of Antiquities in Edinburgh. At Ardestie, two miles north of the village, is a vitrified Iron Age fort and close by a cluster of earth dwellings dating from the 1st century.

West Haven

Carnoustie's name is said to mean 'The Cairn of Heroes' and refers to a semi-mythical battle fought there in 1010 between Malcolm II ('Canmore') and the Danes. The town itself is relatively new, having sprung up in the 20th century as a golfing centre adjacent to the tiny port of West Haven.

Neither **West Haven** nor its sister hamlet **East Haven**, two miles up the coast, have ever had piers, and their harbours are really no more than openings among the rocks. There were, however, communities of fisher-folk at both places for very many years.

In 1855 there were 35 fishermen in the two villages, running 19 small boats and catching lobsters for the London market and crabs for sale locally. Smacks would put into the villages every two or three weeks during the season to transport the shellfish south, and during the winter months the fishermen caught haddock and cod on small-lines — the former for sale at Dundee; the latter for salting down and shipping abroad.

Although there is no commercial fishing from either hamlet today, there is a coastguard station at West Haven and both places are imbued with the atmosphere of fishing and the sea. The old fishers' cottages are still there, and the muddy beaches up which the boats were hauled in bad weather remind one of what the place must have been like a hundred years ago.

From the sea the ruins of the old abbey are very conspicuous as one approaches **Arbroath**, and for many years a lamp was lit behind the great window of the south transept, facing out to sea and known to fishermen as 'The Round O', to guide them into the harbour.

The abbey has a long and distinguished history and the monks played an important part in the growth of fishing in the town. It was founded by William the Lion in 1178 and dedicated to St

Thomas à Becket who had been murdered some eight years before. William was later buried in the abbey and, in 1320, Robert the Bruce's secretary and chaplain, Bernard de Linton, who was also Abbot of Arbroath, there drew up the most important document in Scottish history, the Declaration of Arbroath. In form the Declaration is an appeal from the people of Scotland to the Pope, asking him to intervene in the struggle against England: 'It is in truth not for glory, nor riches, nor honours that we are fighting,' it states, 'but for freedom—for that alone, which no honest man gives up but with life itself.'

The Abbey encouraged and supported the local fishermen, both by building the town's first harbour in 1194, with piers of wood, and by buying large quantities of fish and distributing them to the poor. During the Reformation the Abbey was sacked and the prosperity of the fishermen declined drastically. By 1705 there were so few boats fishing from Arbroath that the town tried to encourage a group of fishermen from the village of Auchmithie, further up the coast, to move into the town. The Laird of Auchmithie, Lord Northesk, was not at all happy about this arrangement and appealed to the Lord Advocate. The Court held that the condition of fishers was the same as that of colliers and salters: they were thralled to their masters in the same way as slaves and could not voluntarily transfer their allegiance.

As a warning to the rest, Northesk then imprisoned a number of his 'slaves' in a dungeon, at Red Castle, so horrific that for generations the fishers would plead that 'they would rather be thrown into the sea from Redhead [the headland north of Auchmithe] than be confined in the pit of Red Castle'.

A new stone pier was erected in 1726, but still the number of boats using the harbour remained small: only three in 1772, and only 14 fishermen in the town in 1795, most of whom were employed as pilots.

At last in 1830 a new deal was struck with the fishermen of Auchmithie, in terms of which a group of them would be given land to build on in return for the fishers moving to Arbroath and using the harbour. In fact the fishermen settled at the end of the High Street, in the old part of the town close to the harbour. Still today this is the fishermen's quarter, known as the 'Fit o' the Toon'.

It is here that the famous 'Arbroath Smokies' are made and there are over 20 private backyards behind the cottages where these delicacies can be bought. The whole neighbourhood is redolent with the smell of wood-smoke and cured fish. During the 19th century the number of boats based in Arbroath gradually increased until, at the height of the herring boom, there were 92 in the fleet, employing 150 fishermen. Today there is still an active fleet of about 30 large modern boats using a wide variety of fishing methods — seine-netting for white fish, trawling for prawns, pair-netting for sprats and creel-fishing for lobsters and crabs. Every weekday afternoon there is a fish market and fish merchants gather to buy boxes of fish from the fast-talking and apparently unintelligible auctioneer.

Just south of the harbour is the Signal Tower Museum, formerly used for communication with Bell Rock lighthouse, which has interesting displays concerning the history of fishing in Arbroath and related topics such as sailmaking. A mile inland of Arbroath is the ancient church of **St Vigeans**, perched on top of a steep conical hump and surrounded by antique gravestones, many of which commemorate fisher-folk.

Though much restored over the centuries, St Vigeans is one of the oldest churches in Scotland and parts of the existing building are Norman. That there was an earlier church here is beyond doubt: numerous fragments and three superb, carved Pictish slabs have been found in the church or graveyard and are now housed in the small museum at the foot of the hill. They date from the early 8th century, and one of them, known as the Drosten Cross, contains the only known inscription in the language of the Picts. A cluster of whitewashed cottages perched on an exposed and barren cliff-top with a tiny harbour

Arbroath

Auchmithie

During the war of 1781 this part of the coast was harried by a French privateer, the *Fearnought* of Dunkirk. On 23rd May she came to anchor in the Bay of Arbroath, fired a few shots into the town, and then sent a flag of truce ashore with the following letter:

> *At sea, May twenty-third.*
> Gentlemen, I send these two words to inform you that I will have you bring to the French colour, in less than a quarter of an hour, or I set the town on fire directly; such is the order of my master the King of France I am sent by. Send directly the mair and chiefs of the town to make some agreement with me, or I'll make my duty. It is the will of yours,
> *M le Capitaine Fall*
> To Monsieurs Mair of the town called
> Arbrought, or in his absence, to the
> chief man after him, in Scotland.

The townspeople ignored his threats, armed themselves and 'ordered him to do his worst for they would not gie him a farthing'.

The French commander was furious and fired heavily upon the town for some time. Fortunately, however, this did no harm except for knocking down a few chimney pots, and the only people hurt were those who attempted to pick up the cannonballs and burned their fingers.

150 feet below — such is **Auchmithie**, the village which supplied Arbroath with its fishermen and introduced the famous Arbroath Smokie.

A surprising place for a fishing community, yet there has been one here for hundreds of years, and until modern times many of the ancient traditions and customs of the fisher-folk were strictly preserved and observed.

The harbour was only built in the 1890s and before that the boats had to be dragged up the shingle beach, strewn with large pebbles which were rackoned to be 'excellently adapted for drying fish'. They would put out before dawn, after white fish with small-lines, the men carried through the surf on the backs of their womenfolk to keep their feet dry. They were back by mid-morning, and the whole community would join in to gut, wash, salt and smoke the catch, and then pack the fish into barrels for transportation to Dundee and elsewhere.

Meanwhile the children were set to baiting the hooks for the next day's fishing, with mussels which had been brought from the Tay or the River Eden: 1,000 hooks on each line, with one line for each fisherman.

In 1840 the population of Auchmithie amounted to 280 people, and 12 boats, each with a crew of five, put out from the harbour regularly. By 1855 the number of boats had risen to 33, but after the First World War the place declined, and by 1929 there were only ten boats and 11 fishermen, most of them old men. During the Second World War a stray German mine blew a large hole in the harbour wall and started a decay which has continued ever since. Today the harbour offers little protection, although there are still a couple of cobles fishing lobsters and crabs from it.

In the middle decades of the 18th century it was remarked that many of the fishermen lived 'in very comfortable circumstances in consequence of their successful exertions in the profitable art of smuggling'. The red sandstone cliffs around Auchmithie are honeycombed with caves — ideal for hiding contraband — and the smuggling activity of the village was immortalised by Sir Walter Scott when he used it as a model for the village of Musselcraig in *The Antiquary*.

In 1970 the Auchmithie Housing Association was set up by the people of the village to restore cottages and harmonise new housing developments in order to save the character of the place. It has been a great success and has avoided the over-precious restoration which has destroyed the authenticity of so many villages. Today 'the straggling street of fishers' cottages' is popular with walkers and birdwatchers.

Beyond Auchmithie, the red sandstone cliffs — often up to 250 feet high and almost precipitous — continue round Red Head into Lunan Bay, where sandy beaches arc northwards.

'The women's dress is, I believe, as worn in Auchmithie, peculiar to that community. Their understandings are wrapped in four or five blue flannel petticoats; these petticoats are so arranged in pleats that they form a rest behind for the creel which contains the haddock, cod, ling, turbot, fluke and skate which they carry far to the inland towns for sale.

'On the upper part of their person they wear short gowns; on their feet stout shoes; and their stalwart legs, which are exposed nearly up to the knee, are encased in coarse worsted stockings. In this unique costume they look very antique and picturesque.'

Alexander Lowson, 1891

In the south-east corner of the bay is the tiny hamlet of **Ethie Haven**, which was a fishing

'The village of Auchmithie is a straggling street of fishers' cottages, some of them fairly comfortable, but the most of them are mere miserable hovels. Middens are before the door, and the whole place is an indescribable scene of dirt and disorder. Were it not for the fine breeze, laden with ozone, which is nearly always blowing upon it from the ocean, this village, instead of being what it is, a remarkably healthy place, would certainly be a hot-bed of disease.'
Alexander Lowson, 1891

The Chapel of St Skae

Close to the cliff-top
between Boddin and
Usan stands the ruin of
the ancient chapel of St
Skae. The adjacent
graveyard is littered
with old carved grave-
stones, many of which
are those of seafarers
from both Boddin and
Usan.

community of some importance in the 18th century but which had declined dramatically by 1845 when the 'New Statistical Account' commented that 'the young men are now seeking employment elsewhere and the old men are afraid to go to sea'. Today the restored fishers' cottages are all holiday homes.

Salmon are still caught there, however, and right up Lunan Bay. From the ruins of the dread Red Castle, commanding the bay from a steep hillock at the mouth of the River Lunan, stake nets can be seen laid out over the wide white sands, and below are a cluster of poles and lines on which the nets are dried and checked. Dunes stretch for nearly four miles north and south and the river, which lures the salmon into the bay, twists below the castle.

Half a mile south of Boddin Point the cliffs start again, though the hamlet of **Boddin** itself is situated beside a small promontory with a sizeable lime-kiln at its point. The village comprises only four houses and a farm, though a number of ruined cottages stand witness to the importance of the ancient lime manufactory. Lime was once exported from here in large quantities and there are still traces of a quay capable of accommodating sizeable vessels at high water.

Beneath the quay is a tiny sandy beach — the only sign of sand between here and Lunan Bay — and it was here that the fishermen ran their boats ashore. One salmon coble uses the harbour today, and the system of ropes and blocks which run it up the slipway demonstrate how it was possible for a number of boats to use the tiny beach in days gone by.

Boddin is a salmon station, and to fish the coast between Lunan Bay and Usan the salmon fisherman must have 11 nets in the sea and another 11 drying on the green beside the harbour. It is an expensive and risky occupation: one storm can destroy half the nets, and each costs £300.

Fishtown of Usan is also a salmon station, and its row of 12 derelict cottages stands above what was once a thriving port. A quarter of the way down the row is a conspicuous square tower, formerly a coastguard station, and beneath it is the shed where the rescue equipment was kept: the rails on which the rockets and lines and breeches buoy were run out are still apparent.

Agates and other semi-precious stones can be found on the boat-strand beneath the village, and at one end of the beach is an ancient vaulted ice-house, with a quay alongside it, reached from the sea by a narrow natural channel through the rocks. At one time there were cottages even here. Ice would arrive from Norway to be loaded into the thick-walled building through a hatch in its roof, and boats would arrive from some distance to fill their holds.

In the 1930s the owner of the village required his

tenants to buy their homes (for £40 each) or get out. The fishers could not afford it, so their landlord blocked the village well and they were forced to emigrate to other villages, mainly to Ferryden near Montrose.

Round the headland from Fishtown of Usan, and still on the Usan Estate, is a small beach known as 'St Mary's Well' after the tiny roofless chapel which stands by the shore.

There was never a fishing community here as such — the large group of derelict buildings nearby was a mill — and the only signs that the beach was a boat-strand are the cleared channel through the rocks and the rusting winches on the foreshore: the wooden shed surrounded by lobster pots and boxes shows that the place is still in use.

A mile beyond Usan the rocky coastline ends in Scurdie Ness, with a lighthouse marking it, and immediately north of this is the mouth of the River South Esk, with Ferryden and Montrose on either side.

At first sight **Ferryden** appears to be a suburb of Montrose: in fact it has long been separate in character and organisation, and its terraced fishers' cottages, many of them restored and modernised, are unlike anything to be found across the river.

There is no commercial fishing done from Ferryden today, and over the last ten years the seafront has been transformed by the North Sea oil industry. Over 30 acres of foreshore between the village and Rossie Island, including the old harbour, has been reclaimed to provide land for an oil rig supply base. In the mid-19th century Ferryden was one of the most important fishing harbours along this stretch of coast: there was a fleet of 25 boats based there and over 200 men were employed at the fishing. Halibut, skate,

cod, ling and haddock were all landed for the market at Montrose, and in the summer months it was not uncommon for the larger boats to land a thousand haddocks after 12-14 hours at sea. They fetched a farthing a pound and were sold to 'cadgers' who would take them to Forfar, Perth and Cupar for resale. During the 1840s it was usual for at least 12 carts laden with haddock to leave Ferryden every day for Dundee.

Then, in the 1920s, the fishing suddenly declined. Investigating the reason for this in 1929, Peter Anson asked local fishermen: 'They will tell you that the harbour is bad, and that there is always the sandbar at the entrance. They will remind you that the fishing grounds are too far off, and are better nearer Gourdon or Arbroath. Yet on the other hand bait is plentiful at Montrose. In bygone days, vessels came here for mussels from as far off as Buckie and Macduff. But since the war social conditions have changed. It is seldom that any of the boys or young men here can be persuaded to go to sea. And the young women of today do not know how to bait lines. . . .'

Across the river from Ferryden is **Montrose** almost surrounded by salt water, with the sea to the east, the River North Esk to the south, and the two square miles of tidal mud flats which make up the Montrose Basin to the west. The town is said to have to have been raised from the sea by the flourish of a wizard's wand.

Records show that there was a town on the site as early as 980 A.D., when it was raided by the Danes, and King William the Lion built a royal castle there, in which he stayed from time to time between 1178 and 1198. The first harbour was built in the Middle Ages, and around it sprang up granaries, warehouses, shipyards and a Customs House. Trade was mainly conducted with Scandinavia, and still is today, for the port

Smuggling in Montrose

Montrose was once the centre of a thriving smuggling trade. It was comparatively remote and had plenty of trade connections with Europe, and since there was strong Jacobite sympathy in most of the townsfolk nobody felt it wrong to defraud the Customs and Excise. There were also any number of willing fishermen to ferry the contraband ashore.

To the north was eight miles of bleak and rocky coast, and to the south the shore between Scurdy Ness and Boddin Point was rich with caves. Wide sandy bays such as Lunan and the five-mile stretch of beach from Montrose to St Cyrus were the delight of smugglers.

Local Customs staff were hopelessly under strength — in the mid-18th century there were only 15 officers to patrol the 25 miles between Montrose and Johnshaven and do all the paperwork forby. The smugglers could more or less do as they pleased, and sometimes chose to smuggle contraband directly into Montrose itself.

A tidesman waiting for the ferry one morning was amazed to see dozens of hogsheads of wine being carried ashore from the ferryboat itself: that haul was enough to fill 3,000 bottles, and the contraband was fine French wine. On another occasion 2,000 gallons of brandy were siezed in the town.

Montrose

is still busy, giving the town a prosperous cosmopolitan air.

James Boswell visited Montrose in 1773 with Dr Samuel Johnson. He wrote: 'We went to see the town-hall, where is a good dancing room and other rooms for tea drinking. The appearance of the town from it is very well: but many of the houses are built with their ends to the street, which looks awkward.'

Houses on the original High Street of Montrose, demolished in 1748, were also built end-on to the street, and this gave the people of the town the nickname 'Gable-enders'.

In the 17th and 18th centuries the Montrose fisheries were of considerable importance, and one of the principal exports to the continent was dried fish: between 1750 and 1776, fifty to a hundred barrels of herring were exported annually to the Baltic, Hamburg, Holland and France. In the latter part of the 19th century the people of Montrose seem to have abandoned fishing altogether, and although there was a brief revival immediately after the First World War, when the Montrose Fishing Company ran a small fleet of steam trawlers, this was dispersed in 1921, and today there are only a handful of fishing boats using the port as a base.

The most lucrative form of fishing carried on from Montrose is that for salmon. The town is the administrative centre for the East Coast Salmon Fishing Industry, and controls the stake-net fishing south to Lunan Bay and north to Charleton and Kinnaber.

The Bruce's Heart
Sir James Douglas, Robert the Bruce's trusted companion throughout the Wars of Independence, vowed he would bear the King's heart to the Holy Land in expiation of Bruce's awful crime of murdering the Red Comyn in a church.

Douglas embarked on this pilgrimage from Montrose in 1330 and reached the Holy Land two years later, where he was killed in battle against the Saracens. The heart was found on the battlefield in its silver casket and returned to Scotland to be buried in Melrose.

THE MEARNS

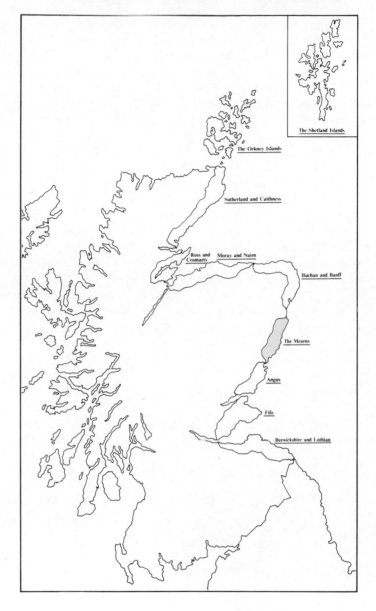

The Shetland Islands

The Orkney Islands

Sutherland and Caithness

Ross and Cromarty Moray and Nairn

Buchan and Banff

The Mearns

Angus

Fife

Berwickshire and Lothian

The district known colloquially as 'The Mearns' is the former County of Kincardine and its coast runs from the north bank of the River South Esk at Montrose to the south bank of the River Dee at Aberdeen. For convenience the City of Aberdeen has been included in this section, though it should, strictly speaking, be part of the next chapter.

The name 'Mearns' derives from Mernia, the brother (and murderer) of King Kenneth II (971-995), who was Mormaer or High Steward of the district. The 'men o' the Mearns' have long had a reputation for skill and strength — a reputation which is summed up by the Scots proverb: 'I can dae fat I dow: the men o' the Mearns can dae nae mair'.

There are still over half a dozen important fishing ports on the Mearns coast, and in days gone by there were many more, yet the coastline does not lend itself to the creation of ports and harbours. It is open and exposed to the prevailing east wind. There is no shelter to be had from offshore islands; there are few coves or gentle bays, and where there are small estuaries they are often treacherous with sand and silt. Along much of its length the coast is a bulwark of fissured sandstone cliffs, inhospitable and dangerous, and in other places the rock gives way to great open strands, windswept and washed by the rolling grey sea.

There is curious marriage custom in St Cyrus instituted by John Orr of Bridgeton, a local laird who left £1,000 in 1847 to provide dowries each year for four brides — the tallest, shortest, oldest and youngest. The minister has to quiz and measure every bride at every wedding.

Gourdon

The original village of **St Cyrus** grew up around the mouth of the River North Esk and was called Ecclescraig. It was engulfed by the sea in a terrible storm in 1795 and the modern village is an amalgamation of the hamlets of Kirkton, Burnside and St Cyrus.

There is an active salmon fishery below the village on the white sands of the northern part of Montrose Bay, and behind it the 'Kairn of Mathers', a medieval tower, is used as a landmark by fishermen. The 'Kairn' was built in 1421 by Lord Barclay to escape the King's vengeance for having killed and 'suppit in bree' (literally 'drank in soup') the Sheriff of the Mearns.

At the pierhead in Gourdon is a public barometer with a somewhat antiquated appearance, in memory of Lieutenant William Farquhar, R.N., drowned far away from this rockbound coast, in the China Sea last century, aged 24.

Beyond the St Cyrus salmon fishery, the coast rises up to the grassy promontory of Milton Ness, on the north-east point of which there used to be a sizeable fishing community.

In 1781 there were 46 families living at **Milton**, 170 souls all told, fishing three boats. A landslip did much damage in 1792, and the village was abandoned by most of its inhabitants: in 1881 there were only eight fishermen here, though there were still four boats. Today the only sign of the former community is the landing-place among the rocks.

Common Surnames

Johnshaven—Blues, McBay.
Gourdon—Criggie, Gove, Gouk.
Cowie—Leiper, Johnstone, Christie.

Two miles further on is the larger village of **Johnshaven**, straggling along the coast for nearly a mile in tightly packed terraces, confined by the steep brae which rises up behind.

The harbour here was built in the early 19th century, with an outer and inner basin, but the fishing from Johnshaven has fluctuated over the years. In 1850 there were 47 boats and 118 fishermen; by 1880 there were 59 boats and 120 fishermen, and in the town's heyday, just before the Great War, 30 or 40 large drifters sailed in search of the herring during the summer months. "Then came the most startling collapse. There are now only three large motor-boats here, used for the great lines, and 20 small yawls. No boy has gone to sea from here for the past 15 years, and in no crew is there a man under 30". (P. F. Anson, 1929)

The number of boats working out of Johnshaven increased between 1930 and 1948, and many of the local fishermen had shares in two boats — a large one for winter fishing off the Yorkshire coast, and a small one for local fishing during the summer. Today, although there is only one boat based there — fishing for lobsters and crabs — Johnshaven provides a base for one of Britain's largest lobster dealers, Murray McBay.

Johnshaven and **Gourdon**, three miles north, were the first villages in Scotland to adopt diesel-powered fishing boats in place of the old steam drifters, and today Gourdon is the only village which still uses the old long-line method of fishing to catch haddock and cod.

As in days gone by, it is the women's job to bait the 1,200 hooks of each line before their men put to sea. Mussels are the bait, and the procedure is known as 'redding'; a way of life that has persisted since time immemorial. The only difference today is that the lines themselves are now made of synthetic fibres rather than flax. There are five active boats working in this way, and another five using modern methods.

Not far offshore are excellent fishing grounds

Johnshaven was notorious in the old days for the activities of the press gangs. The Rev. James Glen, writing in the New Statistical Account 1845), informs us that the fisheries here were formerly much more extensive, but had declined owing to the great depletion of the seafaring population, due to the press gangs in the Napoleonic Wars'.

He went on to consider how his seafaring parishioners were being led astray by the 'most pernicious influence on morals of no less than ten alehouses . . . I cannot say, from personal observation, that there are many people of eminent piety among the fisherfolk'.

On the 4th May 1341, David II and his Queen, Johanna, made forced landing on the promontory of Bervie Brow, returning from nine years' exile in France; their ship had been driven ashore in a storm after evading English pursuit. The King's Step, a nearby boulder, is said to be the actual spot where he first set foot in Scotland again.

At the north end of the main street, close to the bridge, at Inverbervie, is a handsome memorial to Hercules Linton, the designer of the *Cutty Sark*, who was born in the town.

Inverbervie, unlike most coastal burghs which supported the Jacobites, was spared the ravages of the 'Bloody Butcher' (the Duke of Cumberland) after the collapse of the 1745 rising, because the parish minister, with great diplomacy, entertained him at his manse and persuaded him otherwise.

and a market is held in Gourdon every weekday afternoon, depending on the tide. The town also has a sizeable fish-curing business.

Gourdon harbour cost £2,000 when it was built in about 1820. The earlier harbour was very cramped, only holding eight or nine boats, which limited the amount of fishing that could be carried on from there (in 1760 there were only three boats based there though they each had a crew of ten men). Then, after a great storm in 1782, the haddock disappeared entirely from the neighbouring fishing grounds. The harbour has a sheltered inner basin, protected by a wooden gate which is closed in bad weather. Halfway up the hill, behind it, is a beacon, not unlike a small lighthouse, for the boats to take a fix on when they are entering Gourdon in the dark. Today the town is a growing sea-angling centre.

In spite of being an ancient royal burgh, there is little sign of the past in the small industrial town of **Inverbervie**, where the first machine for spinning linen in Scotland was set up in 1788.

The shore below the town is piled high with millions of sea-washed pebbles, among them agates, jasper, serpentine and cornelians. The roar that the pebbles make on a stormy day with a good swell rolling in will not be forgotten easily.

There is a small salmon station on the beach, but this is all that remains of a fishing industry that once employed over 70 men. In the middle decades of the last century large quantities of cod and ling were landed at Bervie and salted down for the London market, about one hundred barrels being taken annually to Montrose for

shipping south. Bervie haddocks were renowned in Glasgow, and for a time during the late 18th century there was some herring fishing from here, but by the end of the century the herring had entirely disappeared from the Kincardine-shire coast.

The coastline between Johnshaven and Inver-bervie is made up of low rocky ledges and grassy braes: from Craig David, just north of Bervie Bay, right up to Stonehaven, some nine miles away, the sea breaks against steep cliffs.

Even on such an inhospitable coastline, fishing communities managed to survive in days gone by. At Shieldhill (known formerly as Kinneff Haven), Catterline and Crawton, the villages cling to the tops of the cliffs — the 'heugh-heid' as it is known on the East Coast — with their tiny harbours below.

Old Church Kinneff

Charles II was crowned King of Scots on New Year's Day 1651, ten years before he ascended the Throne of England, and after the coronation the Scottish regalia were taken to Dunnottar Castle for safety, along with some private papers belonging to the King.

Knowing this, a Parliamentarian army under General Overton besieged the castle for eight months, but in the meantime the Crown (which had been made for Robert the Bruce), the Sword of State and the Sceptre of Scotland, had been smuggled out by the wife of the minister of Kinneff Kirk. She took them to Kinneff and for some time they were hidden under the pulpit of the old church.

With its freshly painted rows of white cottages, **Catterline** is one of the best preserved of all the 'heugh-heid' villages. It stands some three-quarters of a mile beyond Tod Head lighthouse — the most powerful light between Scurdy Ness and Aberdeen — visible for 17 miles.

The village was first recorded as 'Katerlin' in the 12th century, and there are remains of an ancient church dedicated to St Catherine in the kirkyard. For many centuries the village was inhabited by fisherfolk, though it was never an important fishing station: the New Statistical Account of 1845 mentions merely that 'smuggling has been suppressed' and makes a tantalising reference to 'drunkenness, theft and perjury'. At that time there were nine boats there and 22 fishermen: by 1881 the number of men had risen to 30 and eight boats sailed annually to the summer herring fishing. Like so many places, the number of boats declined after the First World War, but the pier — which was built by Viscount Arbuthnot in about 1810 — is still used for landing salmon, and there remains one handsome lobster boat working from it.

In modern times Catterline was celebrated by the great artist Joan Eardley who lived here for many years and died there in 1963.

Catterline had a sister village a mile away at

On 10th February 1891, the liner *Bravo* and the Scarborough smack *Northern Belle* collided at sea. The *Northern Belle* ran aground at Whistleberry near Kinneff, after she had passed through a fleet of fishing boats. The fishermen saw no one aboard her and, on examination, Lieutenant Barnard found no trace of a collision. Michael Holmes, coastguard of Catterline, said no one from the fishing or farming community would go near her, regarding her as a 'phantom ship'.

Catterline gives its name to an unusual kind of lobster-pot that is covered with wooden slats instead of netting.

In 1645, the Seventh Earl Marischal, a stubborn Covenanter, withstood a siege by Montrose in Dunottar Castle. In revenge, Montrose wasted the country for miles around and burned the town of Stonehaven; the Chronicler records that the country was 'uterlie spoilzeit, plunderit and undone'. In 1685 the castle was the prison of 167 Covenanters, including 45 women, who were held in the grim Whigs' Vault.
    In the churchyard of Dunottar, Sir Walter Scott met for the first and last time Robert Paterson, the original 'Old Mortality', cleaning the headstones of the graves of those Covenanters who died in Dunottar Castle.

Along the High Street in Stonehaven, at midnight on Hogmanay, the young men of the burgh take part in the ceremony known as 'swinging the fireballs'. This dates back to pagan times when fireballs were swung around in order to ward off evil spirits.

Aberdeen Trawler Crew

Dunnottar Castle

Crawton, but where the former has continued to survive, albeit in reduced circumstances, the latter was abandoned by the fishers in the 1920s.

There was never any pier or sheltered harbour on the beach below, for one thing, and as the inshore fishing became less plentiful the community had no alternative but to emigrate: the last family left in 1926 and today the houses are all ruined and the path down to the beach overgrown. A place of ghosts, its only inhabitants today are the numerous fulmars and herring gulls which nest in the cliffs above the old boat-strand.

The first harbour at **Stonehaven** was established by the Fifth Earl Marischal in the early 16th century and what is today referred to as the 'Old Town' grew up around it. The place was originally named 'Stanehive' — the 'stane' or 'stone' being a great boulder known as '*Craig-na-caer*' which rose from the sea at the entrance to the harbour — a considerable danger to shipping until it was dynamited in 1816 by Robert Stevenson, the famous engineer who was Robert Louis Stevenson's grandfather.

In the early 19th century a 'New Town' was laid out above the existing port. It became the residential quarter for the merchants and professional people, but even at the height of Stonehaven's prosperity in the 1880s the fisherfolk preferred to live in the Old Town. Today this part still has the feel of a medieval township, though little remains of the original buildings except the Tolbooth close to the harbour (now an excellent local museum): Stonehaven was sacked by Montrose in 1645, again by General Monk in 1657 and finally by the Duke of Cumberland in 1746.

Stonehaven developed largely as a fishing town, though its history as such has been chequered. The Old Statistical Account (1791-99) says that there were only three boats and one yawl working from there, and that the fishermen's 'morals were being ruined through excessive drinking of spirits': the New Statistical Account (1845) mentions only five or six boats. This is surprising as Stonehaven is the best harbour between Arbroath and Aberdeen and, during the herring boom in the 1880s, the port came into its own, with a fleet of almost a hundred boats. With the end of the herring boom the town again went into decline. Aberdeen's phenomenal

At Stonehaven in 1748 three Jacobite Episcopalian clergymen were interned in the Tolbooth for six months by the Presbyterians. During this time, fishermen's wives from the coastal havens would trudge along the sea-beach with creels on their backs concealing babies to be baptised by the gaoled pastors, who extended their hands through the stanchioned windows. This scene is depicted by S. W. Brownlow in a famous painting made in 1865.

Robert William Thomson, inventor of the pneumatic tyre, was born in 1822 on the south side of the town square in Stonehaven.

Muchalls Castle, dating from 1619, is a complete example of a 17th century Scottish laird's home. It has handsome plaster ceilings, rivalling those at Glamis and Cragievar, a secret staircase, a Green Lady and a wishing well in the courtyard; it used to have a tunnel which led to a smugglers' cave known as Gin Shore. This was blocked on the orders of a Lord Justice General of Scotland who lived in the castle in the 19th century, when the old fishing village Stranathro was replaced by the present 'model' one. However, the development of new trawling techniques in Aberdeen lured most of the villagers away before building was completed.

prosperity during the later years of the 19th century must have been largely responsible for this, and the fact that Stonehaven harbour was liable to silting made it unsuitable for large boats and contributed to its decline. Today there are five trawlers, one seine-netter and seven crab boats (the lobsters have all but died out) fishing from Stonehaven and another half dozen Stonehaven boats work out of Aberdeen. The place has a growing reputation as a sea-angling centre, and on the pier-head is Robert Gordon's Institute of Technology's deep sea rescue research establishment.

As the road climbs out of Stonehaven to the north it overlooks **Cowie** village with its tiny harbour and rows of fishers' cottages — 'Boaty Row', 'Helen Row' and 'Amy Row'.

Today Cowie is connected to Stonehaven by a promenade, but in the Middle Ages it was a Royal Burgh, with its own castle built by Malcolm Canmore in the 11th century (some vestiges of which remain on a rock above the shore). During the 1850s there was a larger fleet of boats there than at Stonehaven (23 in 1850, employing 62 fishermen; to Stonehaven's 11 boats, employing 17 men in all).

In 1864 cholera visited the village with the survivors of a Swedish wreck and claimed so many victims among the fisherfolk that the community never regained the same level of porsperity, although there were still 33 small boats there in 1929. Today there is one substantial coble working out of the semi-ruined harbour, and at the end of the village is a green for drying stake nets.

The coastline between Stonehaven and Aberdeen — a distance of about ten miles — is one of almost perpendicular cliffs topped by grassy braes and broken here and there by tiny coves or bays. Six small fishing communities grew up along this rugged shore, all of them 'heugh-heid' villages with their tiny boat-strands or harbours on the shore below.

The southernmost is **Muchalls**, a 'model' village built in 1865 to replace the ancient hamlet of Stranathra, and popular today as a commuter base for Aberdeen. Most of the fine old cottages have been well restored, and a village twice the size of the original one has sprung up behind them.

Newtonhill, or Skateraw as it was formerly known, is another village which would probably have become a cluster of ruins had it not been for its proximity to Aberdeen. The old fishers' cottages have all been over-restored and the village has grown into a township of modern private houses built by city-folk attracted by the superb view of the sea.

Today the pier is in ruins, though in the 1850s haddock, cod and ling were landed here in great quantities. Haddock were sold fresh locally or

Fishwife

dried in the sun to become 'spelding'. The smoke-curing of 'Findon haddocks' was also done in most of the cottages. Fishing died out here with the advent of the steam drifter and the steam trawler.

Fish Curing in the North-East

Throughout the north-east, excess fish was carried inland and sold or bartered for eggs, butter, cheese and oatmeal. This still did not get rid of all the fish, however, and from an early date the surplus was cured by a variety of methods.

One of the earliest methods was that of air-drying into 'spelding'. Haddocks were gutted and split with their heads left on, soaked in strong brine and laid on smooth pebbles on the beach. If the weather was fair they were left there for several days to harden, occasionally being flattened by pressing with flat stones. The drying process took about a week and the result was a hard, greenish-red fish. The work was, of course, all done by the womenfolk, who would then take some of the spelding and hang them in the chimney or over the peat fire, and the result was known as a 'Findrum' or 'Boddam' cure (after the villages of the same names). The spelding, findrums or boddams could now be transported with ease and found their way as far south as London.

The other major type of curing developed in the north-east was salt pickling herrings. The process had been perfected by the Dutch in the 14th century and Dutch curers had come to Aberdeenshire to show their method, known as 'Peekle Herring'.

A popular dish in the area when food was scarce was to soak and then boil dried cod and ling and flake it into some mashed potatoes. The flakes of fish resemble fine hairs, and because of this the dish was known as 'hairy tatties'.

In the 19th century a change took place in fish-eating habits, spurred on by three factors: the railways, the use of ice and refrigeration and steam trawling. It was no longer necessary to create a non-perishable commodity, but the old tradition was not neglected and the cures were modified to make them more palatable — hence the development of the kipper and the finnan haddock.

Having sought out the handful of original fishers' cottages at **Downies** among the mass of new bungalows, the grassy track leading to the shore seems to head straight over the edge of the cliff, and if it was not for two rusted winches far below, it would seem to have been an impossible place to fish from.

Not only is the beach only a few yards long and the shore rough and stony, but the bank up which the boats had to be hauled is very steep. On both sides of the tiny cove rise high, grass-covered stacks; there are ugly looking rocks everywhere and the place seems a most unlikely site for a harbour.

Because of the difficulty in linking both Downies and **Portlethen** to the mains water and sewerage systems, the local residents dug their heels in and demanded that these modern conveniences be supplied, and they won their case. Today both villages are popular with Aberdeen commuters. Portlethen beach is only slightly less formidable than Downies' and the steep bank which is the boat-strand is still crowded with small boats. The harbour is a salmon station and above it is a drying green for stake nets.

A mile beyond Portlethen is the village of **Findon**, famous as the birthplace of the 'finnan haddie'. Findon haddocks were split, dried and cured over peat smoke, and by the end of the 18th century they were 'known and esteemed in most parts of Scotland'. In the 1870s, however, the Factory Acts insisted that all the Findon haddocks should be smoked in modern fish-houses under strict rules of hygiene, so no finnan haddies have in fact been made at Findon for over a century.

The village was never an important fishing station, and as at Portlethen and Downies the boats were winched up beyond the high-water mark onto the grassy banks above the shingle by means of windlasses and wooden slipways.

Mostly inshore fishing was executed in Portlethen. The New Statistical Account (1845) remarks that the 'plausible pretext for the great number of public houses in the village is its situation on a rocky coast where wrecks sometimes occur'.

As far back as the 14th century there were harbour works in Aberdeen, and in 1610 a notable hazard to navigation, a rock called Craig Metallan, was removed by the now famous David Anderson, thereafter known as 'David do a'thing'.

Findon Fish Pudding

This recipe was scrawled on a scrap of paper among the pages of an old cookery book from this area and described as 'very convenient'.
2 lbs potatoes
1¼ lbs fillets
1 oz butter
2 tbsps milk or cream
topping—1 tomato
—grated cheese

2 lbs potatoes
1¼ lbs fillets of haddock
1 oz butter
2 tbsps milk or cream
topping–1 tomato/grated cheese

Preheat the oven to 350°F/Gas Mark 4. Peel the potatoes and boil them. While they boil, put the fish onto a greased baking tray, dot with butter and sprinkle with milk. Cover with foil and bake for 20 minutes. Remove from the oven and leave to cool. Now wash the potatoes, drain the cooking stock from the fish into them and then flake the fish on top. Mash this all together and season well. Put onto a greased 2½ pint pie dish. Arrange sliced tomato on top and cover with cheese. Heat in the oven and serve with leeks in a cream sauce.

Cove harbour uses a natural rock formation as a breakwater and, unusually for heugh-heid hamlets, is linked to its village by a road. The harbour is still used by about 20 lobster boats and salmon cobles, and a certain amount of inshore fishing is also done from there. At the height of its prosperity, in the 1880s, there were as many as 96 men and boys engaged in the fishing with a fleet of 30 boats. It is difficult to imagine how all the boats managed to fit into the harbour: in fact they were dragged up onto the grass beyond the beach, as they are today.

From January to May the fishermen would work the 'Long Forties'; well stocked with haddock and comparatively shallow, but plagued with dogfish which destroyed the lines and ate the fish off the hooks.

Aberdeen today is a city in transition. Over the last 20 years its whole outlook has changed as it has adapted itself, first to the loss of the Faroes fishing grounds on which much of its wealth as a fishing port was based, and second to the arrival of the North Sea oil industry.

The harbour is crowded with as many vessels associated with the new industry as with fishing boats, but the port still teems with activities related to fishing — curing sheds, chandlers, fish buyers, and the busy daily market which sold £25,000,000 worth of fish last year (1983).

The city grew up around the medieval harbour, and the improvements made to the port by the famous engineers Smeaton (in the late 18th century) and Telford (in the early 19th century) placed the town among the most important trading ports in the country.

It is somewhat surprising, therefore, that until

Aberdeen

'The beauty of Aberdeen is the beauty of uniformity and solidity, nothing so time-defying has been built since the Temple of Karnak.'
H. V. Morton, 1929

Early in the 19th century in Aberdeen there was a successful smuggling syndicate, Christie and Mitchell, which went so far as to advertise in the *Aberdeen Journal*: 'Quantity of ancker gin . . and a fresh supply daily expected'. This enterprise went bankrupt; the effective, locally based coast-guard putting an end to their daily deliveries.

the 1880s there was relatively little fishing carried on from there.

Large quantities of fish were carried into the market from surrounding villages as far distant as Newburgh, 15 miles to the north. In 1784, John Knox bemoaned this lack of enterprise regarding fishing, writing: 'If the merchants should also export cargoes of fifty or sixty vessels constantly employed in the herring and white fisheries, the port of Aberdeen would, in a few years, become the most celebrated mart of fish now existing.'

Almost one hundred years went by before Knox's prophecy was fulfilled. In 1882 a group of local businessmen formed a syndicate and acquired a steam tugboat called the *Toiler* 'for the purpose of prosecuting trawl fishing'. Local opposition to this scheme was loud and long but the project was an immediate, and phenomenal, success. Within a few years fishing families from scores of villages all round the East Coast of Scotland were moving to Aberdeen to seek their fortunes and, backed by southern money, the fleet of steam trawlers grew and grew: by 1900 there were 205 trawlers fishing from Aberdeen, providing a living for approximately 25,000 people ashore and afloat: by 1930 there were over 270 trawlers and 40 steam liners based there.

At last the great North Sea fishing grounds could be reached, and with the advent of even longer-range trawlers with ice equipment to keep the fish fresh, the massive fishing grounds towards Iceland and the Arctic Circle were opened up. Aberdeen became one of the most important fishing ports in the world.

Aberdeen Whiting

8 small whole whiting
seasoned flour
2 oz butter
chopped parsley
chopped chives
¼ pint milk
2 tbsps cream

Clean and gut the fish. Flour them and fry them in butter, slowly, without browning. Chop up the parsley and chives finely. Add to milk and cream, mix thoroughly and pour over the whiting before they are wholly cooked. Serve with boiled potatoes.

Today there are only 49 vessels indigenous to Aberdeen, although 50 or 60 'strangers' from Fife, Buckie or Peterhead use the port regularly, and at times there are many more boats landing fish there. Most of the boats are between 60 and 80 feet in length — the most efficient size for the mixed coaster and deep sea fishing that the majority of the boats pursue: the days of the large deep sea trawlers went with the loss of the deep sea fishing grounds in the 1960s.

At the head of the North Pier in the heart of Aberdeen is the village of **Footdee** or 'Fittie', laid out in the early 19th century at the mouth (or 'foot') of the River Dee. Originally plans were drawn up for buildings of two storeys, but the fisherfolk refused absolutely to live above stairs and insisted on having earthen floors. They got their way and the City Architect laid out the 'village' in three squares, with neither doors nor windows in the outside walls, so that the fisherfolk could be completely isolated from the public gaze, and safe from the sea during times of flood. At the end of the 19th century the population of Footdee was 584, which amounted to nine people in each two-roomed cottage. In some cases there were two families in a single room, and there were 54 families within the three small squares. Originally the menfolk were pilots and lifeboatmen in Aberdeen harbour, but with the herring boom they returned to fishing. They were generally much poorer than the rest of their brethren, with older boats which could not venture far from shore.

BUCHAN
AND BANFF

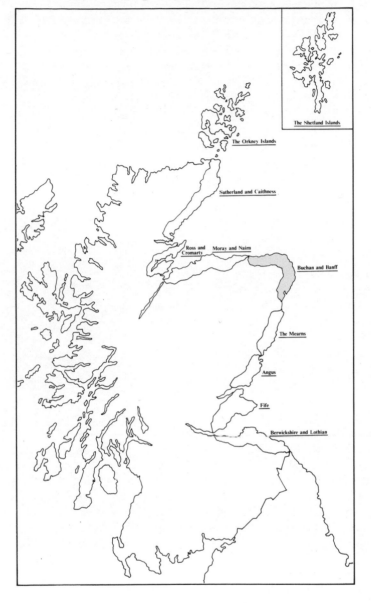

The great shoulder of land which is the North East of Scotland juts far out into the North Sea, its coast closer than any other part of the British mainland to the plentiful offshore fishing grounds towards Norway and Iceland. The area has been rich in fishing communities from early times — in about 1800 there were over 70 distinct communities along this stretch of coastline, and still today there are over 40, among them the busiest fishing port in Europe and some of the most picturesque villages on the entire east coast.

The situation and prosperity (or otherwise) of the villages of Buchan and Banff owes much to the attitudes of local landowners. Every acre of the rolling arable and pasture land was used to grow crops or fatten beasts, and often fishing communities were given narrow strips on which to set up their homes, places which were agriculturally worthless. In other places landlords built fine harbours and encouraged the fishing in many other ways.

Beyond the Bridge of Don just north of the City of Aberdeen, the coast levels out for about ten miles into spacious beaches backed by rich farmland as far as the mouth of the River Ythan which winds through the vast dunes of the Sands of Forvie Nature Reserve.

A mile up river lies the sizeable village of **Newburgh**, at one time a fishing station of some importance, though one of the few signs of the trade still visible today is an old vaulted ice-house, used for the storage of fish. The low peninsula which juts from the village out into the estuary is called the Inch and its end is a fish curing warehouse and a small ruined building which was formerly a mussel store. Mussels — used as bait by line fishermen — were abundant on the shore here. Most of the gravestones in the old graveyard on the Inch commemorate ship masters, ships' engineers, pilot masters and so on.

During the winter the Fittie men used to lay up their bigger sailing boats here, and in 1880 there were 11 boats fishing out of Newburgh, local fisherwives taking the catch to Aberdeen daily. Besides salmon, sea and lake trout, and pike, the River Ythan contains pearl mussels. One of the largest pearls in the ancient crown of Scotland was obtained from this stream.

The harbour at Newburgh is tidal, and the first good harbour north of Aberdeen is at **Collieston**, two miles further on, where the sand dunes give way to a deep rocky bay called St Catherine's Dub. The bay received this unusual name after a Flemish galleon of the same name was wrecked there in 1594 with a cargo of arms to aid the Catholic rebellion led by the Earls of Errol and Huntly. Various relics have been raised from the wreck and divers still prospect there.

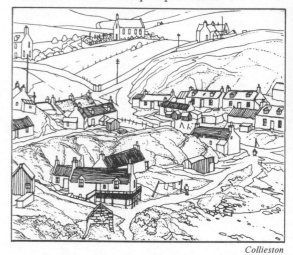

Collieston

A pier was built at the village exactly three hundred years later because the fishing was prospering to such an extent. At this time there were over 60 boats there, employing 170 fishermen: it was even proposed that a branch railway line be run into the village, but the boom petered out as the small boats were outmoded and the young men joined larger boats elsewhere.

A strong, curving breakwater protects a sandy bay surrounded by grassy braes. Some of the fishermen's houses cluster close to the beach, others stand on top of the brae: many of them are holiday cottages today, but they have been well restored and there is nothing here to spoil the charm of this picturesque spot.

The Lang Reel o' Collieston

A curious custom attended the fishers' weddings at Collieston. After the service a banquet was enjoyed by the whole community and then they would repair to the links at the end of Forvie Sands to dance the intricate 'Lang Reel o' Collieston' to the strains of fiddles. The reel would be opened by the bride and groom, and then the whole community would join in, in pairs, and then drop out again until only the first couple were left.

An author in the Banffshire Journal remarked in 1870 that to see it was 'a treat worth going many miles to enjoy'.

The Old Statistical Account of 1793 says of Newburgh that it is 'a dirty place in pleasant and commodious situation, with six or seven alehouses'. Its population was then under 200!

Newburgh

At fisher weddings in the villages close to Aberdeen it was customary for the youngest members of the boat's crew to carry a large flag into the house, wrap the bride in it and give her a kiss.

A little north of Collieston, standing on a narrow promontory with cliffs which plunge 120 feet sheer into the seething tide, is a hamlet which has been called 'the most curiously situated village on the east coast of Scotland' (P. F. Anson). The fishers' cottages are clustered round the ruins of the **Old Castle of Slains**, an impregnable fortress blown up by James V in person in the early 17th century after the rebellion of the Catholic earls. Dr Johnson remarked that the situation of Slains Castle was 'the noblest he had ever seen . . . better than Mount Edgeecombe, which was reckoned to be the first in England'. Somewhat surprisingly, there were nearly 50 fishermen living on this exposed spot in 1850, fishing from a small shingle beach at the foot of the cliff, reached by a narrow winding track. There are still a couple of decayed corrugated-iron tackle sheds on the beach.

Old Castle of Slains

Two and a half miles further north begins the bite of Cruden Bay, site of a great battle between the Scots and the Danes in 1012, and at the southern end of the bay, overlooking the treacherous Skares rocks, is the village of **Whinnyfold** (pronounced 'Finnyfa'). Now a popular place with holidaymakers, the village has changed little in appearance since the end of its activities as a commercial fishing village. It is laid out in four parallel rows of cottages facing the sea on top of the cliff in the manner of a true 'heugh heid' community. Most of the cottages have been well restored and there are no new

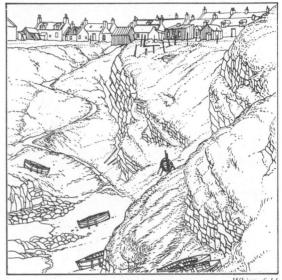

Whinnyfold

'The Crooked Mary'

In the 18th century smuggling was at its height and many Buchan fishermen made a good living by lending a helping hand when there was a 'run'. The most noted lugger engaged in smuggling was the *Crooked Mary* which called at Slains, Cruden and Peterhead. It was the 18th December 1798 and a 'run' was on. The *Crooked Mary* had been sighted off the Buchan coast late in the afternoon and the 'land party' was warned. Just before midnight, therefore, the party, six in number with two carts, greased and padded, were waiting at the little bay just north of Slain's Kirk, where the loading was to take place.

Everything was going well, but the 'gauger' or excise officer had been overlooked. He was a bitter man and relentless in his war against smugglers; he was called Anderson and had two assistants with him that night.

Somehow he had learned a run was on that night and, on the road which led from the bay to the main road, they selected their place of ambush. Soon the muffled carts could be heard approaching and the 'gaugers' fired their pistols, but in the darkness their shots went wide. The horses bolted, and with the exception of Philip Kennedy, the smugglers fled into the night. Kennedy stood his ground and fought back, but the 'guagers' were armed with swords and severely wounded him. They left him lying there where he had fallen.

In the cold light of dawn the fatally wounded smuggler was discovered by friends in the kirkyard of Slains, to which he had dragged himself, beyond help; his last words were, 'If the others had been as true as I, the good would have got through, and I would not be bleeding to death.'

Anderson was afterwards tried and acquitted of murder in 1798. Kennedy's tombstone remains to this day in the crowded graveyard.

At Whinnyfold the favourite bait was lugworms, brought from Ardersier on the west coast. The fishwives could carry these down the almost sheer cliff path in their creels and plant them out in 'scabs' on flat rocks below the high tide mark. When the tide came in the worms would anchor themselves to the rocks, thus providing the fishermen with a living larder.

An early visitor of note who came annually between 1893 and 1910 was Bram Stoker, creator of Dracula.

buildings in the village. The boat strand is on the small shingle beach below, pressed close by rocky headlands and outcrops, and the two old iron winches are still used to haul up small boats.

During the last century the fishwives of Whinnyfold used to walk the 12 miles to Peterhead carrying their creels of fresh fish, and Whinnyfold fish had a reputation even further afield than that: in Edinburgh there was one fishmonger who made a special point of advertising when he had 'The Real Johnny Gray' — haddocks smoked in old Whinnyfold.

At the northern end of **Cruden Bay** is the holiday town of the same name, popular since the 1920s for its acres of magnificent pink beach, backed by high dunes and an excellent links golf course, and adjacent to it is the thriving salmon station of **Port Errol**.

It used to be said that the division between the villages was marked by the Old Kirk: Port Errol stretches in a row of pink stone cottages, at right angles to the beach, and facing it across the mouth of the River Cruden. The village was named after the Earls of Errol whose family seat at Slains Castle stands nearby and who built the harbour itself.

The harbour is just beyond the village, sheltering a number of new salmon cobles and a couple of lobster boats with a large drying green for stake nets close by. The salmon fishings from this

Cruden Bay

station run from the south end of Cruden Bay to Boddam village and have been worked by the same family for three generations.

One of the most dramatic sites on the entire east coast is the great cauldron of the **Bullers of Buchan**. The granite cliffs that front this length of coastline are rugged with little coves and inlets — more 'cracks' than 'creeks' — one of which forms a harbour for the Bullers of Buchan. The village perches above the creek in two tightly packed rows of cottages with their little gardens behind them. The cottages are now mainly

holiday properties and have been somewhat 'over-restored' which detracts from the hamlet's authenticity: pink pebble-dash obscures the pink granite from which most of the cottages are built. There is no question of the boat strand's authenticity, however. Steep cliffs tower on either side of the creek, thronged with kittiwakes, fulmars and shags, and close by is the famous 'Pot', a massive granite amphitheatre where the sea rushes in through an arched tunnel — invisible from both the harbour and the village.

Johnson and Boswell visited the place on 24th August 1773, Boswell remarking that it was 'somewhat horrid to move along' the Pot's narrow outer rim, which in places is only a yard or so wide. Later in the same century a local gentleman, made courageous by drink, accepted a bet that he could gallop round the Pot on horseback. He won the bet, but when he sobered up and realised what he had done, died of a heart attack. . . .

The steep cliffs continue round Buchan Ness, the most easterly point in Scotland. In places they are over 200 feet tall and they have claimed many victims: between November 1816 and March 1819, 20 ships were wrecked there, yet it took two petitions — one in 1819, the other in 1822 — from merchants, shipowners, ship masters and others interested in the sea, to persuade the Commissioners for the Northern Lighthouses to build Buchan Ness lighthouse. Finally the granite tower was built there in 1827.

The village of **Boddam**, just beyond the Ness, and 'in the shadow of' the lighthouse, is also entirely built of pink granite and many of its houses look as if they are newly built, although some of them are 200 years old. The older cottages cluster round the large double harbour and at one time all the streets were lettered — A Street, B Street and so on — except Harbour Street.

According to the 1845 Statistical Account, William of Orange planted a settlement of Dutch fishermen on this part of the coast, and there is a local tradition that the fishers of Boddam are descended from them.

Peterhead was called Peter Ugie until the late 16th century. It is often locally referred to as the Blue Town, the town of the 'blue Mogganers'. This is a reference to the long blue stockings the fishermen used to wear, 'mogan' being Gaelic for boot-stockings.

In its heyday, Boddam supported 151 boats and 476 fishermen, and its collapse in the early decades of this century was sudden — as it was in many fishing villages on the east coast — though a newspaper in 1928 said that 'nowhere is the decline more pronounced or the distress more acute than at Boddam'. The blame was laid on the steam trawlers which proliferated during this period at the expense of the smaller boats which Boddam harboured: more likely it was due to the port's nearness to Peterhead and the growth in the port's importance during this period.

The curing yards and warehouses on the northern side of the harbour were converted by Highland Seafoods into a fish processing factory in about 1950 and this business still thrives. In 1976 the quay was rebuilt in connection with Peterhead Power Station which towers behind the village, and this gave the harbour a new vigour, although the living of the eight full-time lobster boats and 12 part-timers which work from Boddan is threatened by the fact that no limit has been proposed to prevent other boats fishing close in to the shore along this stretch of the coast.

The first harbour at **Peterhead** was built in 1593 and was known as 'Port Henry'. The place had several natural advantages as a shelter, not least the presence of the long rocky islet of Inch Keith, now joined to the mainland by a fine new area of land reclamation, which provides a breakwater and creates a natural harbour. The 16th-century harbour was much used as a place of refuge in bad weather, for the coastline north and south was rocky and treacherous, and it was the second station after the Shetlands for the Dutch fishing 'busses' during this and the following century. At one time the Dutch even tried to buy Inch Keith as a depot.

By the end of the 18th century the old harbour was in disrepair and inadequate for the amount of traffic using it. Several petitions were laid before Parliament for the creation of a 'great harbour', and in 1775 Smeaton, the greatest harbour builder of his day, began work on the existing South Harbour. Telford continued this project after the port had been deepened, and the North Harbour was completed in 1822. To this was added the Alexandra Basin, and there are plans to further extend the South Harbour.

Peterhead owed its first success as a commercial fishing port to the whaling that was carried on from there in the early 19th century. Between 1788, when the industry started, and 1823, when herring fishing took over, the port was the premier whaling station in the whole country with a fleet of 16 ships putting out for months at a time in search of the whale. The Arbuthnot Museum in the town has a good collection of whaling memorabilia.

Herring fishing from Peterhead started only in

Boddam

Peterhead

In 1642 Peterhead was granted a supernatural manifestation and warning: '. . . in a seaman's house at Peterheid there was hard, upone the night, beatting of drums, uther tymes sounding of trumpettis, playing of pifferis and ringing of bellis, to the astoneishment of the heirens. Troubles follouit.'

1818 but developed rapidly. By 1836 there were 262 boats there, and over 40,000 barrels of fish were exported that year. By 1850 the port was the second herring station in all Scotland, with 400 fishing from it and 27 curing establishments in the town. During the herring boom in the 1880s the number of boats rose to 480.

Today Peterhead ranks as the principal fishing port in the whole of Europe. Its own fleet amounts to only 100 boats — mainly middle-range purse and seine-net trawlers between 60 and 80 feet in length (the larger boats tend to use Aberdeen) — but a further 300 boats of the same sort use the port as a base, and the daily fish market handles an average of 50,000 boxes per week, 80% of them haddock and cod, worth £2½ million per annum.

The fish market, which runs along the East Pier and the Alexandra Basin, is 1,250 feet long. At weekends the harbour is crammed with boats of all sizes, and from all over the country, and the sight of the fleet racing out to the fishing grounds at midnight on Sunday is a memorable one.

To the south of the fishing harbour, Peterhead Bay provides shelter for boats associated with the North Sea oil industry and there is a tanker terminal there which can handle ships of up to 40,000 tons. The two sturdy breakwaters that create shelter in Peterhead Bay were built by prisoners from Peterhead Prison in the 1950s.

There are two named 'suburbs' of Peterhead which were formerly fishing villages in their own right: **Roanheads**, by the North Harbour, which was the original fishing town and which contains some well-restored old fishermen's houses; and **Buchanhaven** at the mouth of the River Ugie, to the north-west. Buchanhaven gives the visitor an idea of what Peterhead town would have been like in the mid-19th century. It has its own pier and boat-strand — still used during the summer months for small private boats although there is no proper harbour — and many of its inhabitants still go to the fishing, though from Peterhead now, not from Buchanhaven itself. The oldest house in the 'Blue Toon' is to be found there: a 16th-century fish house, appropriately.

North of Peterhead the white beaches of Rattray Bay are north to Rattray Head, with its light-house warning shipping of the shelving shore and fast-running tide. The old saying was 'Keep Mormond Hill a hand-spike high, and Rattray Briggs ye'll nae come nigh", but today the flame from the North Sea gas terminal at St Fergus adds another beacon to the lighthouse's warning and the coast does not claim many casualties. Sandy beaches continue north-west for a further four miles to Inzie Head, a mile south of which is the vanished hamlet of **Cox Haven**. This village grew up around the small creek at the mouth of

Strathbeg Burn, and in the mid-18th century there was a community of half a dozen families there, all bearing the name Cox. Where they came from, mobody knows, and where they disappeared to is a mystery. It is possible that the community pursued some ancient religious observance, associated with the 'fresh-water dolphins' of Loch Strathbeg, but what is certain is that there are no signs of habitation there now. The other side of Inzie Head are the twin villages of **St Combs** and **Charleston**, and a mile further north the similar pair of **Inverallochy** and **Cairnbulg**.

Each pair of villages is separated by a stream, and neither has a pier, the boats being dragged up onto the beach. The old cottages huddle close to the shore, presenting blank gable-ends to the sea, to keep out the damaging north-east wind, and behind them have sprung up modern bungalows.

Until the 1860s all four villages were motley clusters of rude clay huts, with their middens before their doors. Then cholera struck and it was clear that if the communities were going to survive there had to be a clean-up. Many of the old huts were replaced at this time, and washing at the village pump every evening before bed was made part of the school curriculum.

Between Cairnbulg and Fraserburgh is the impressive pile of Cairnbulg Castle, the home of Lady Saltoun, descendant of the founder of Fraserburgh, and Captain Alexander Ramsay of Mar, a grandson of Queen Victoria.

he people of verallochy and airnbulg hold a assive Temperance arch on New Year's ay.

is unknown when the st fishermen settled Fraserburgh, but P. Anson fixes the date 1789 when a group fishermen moved ere from Broadsea llage as a protest ainst having to pay a x of one-sixth of each at's catch to the local ndowner.

he Old Pretender, mes III and IX, nded at Fraserburgh 1715 to stir up pport for the cobite Rising of that ar.

O impregnable and very ancient rock,
Rejecting the violence of water,
Ignoring its accumulations and strategy,
You yield to history nothing.
(George Bruce, 'Kinnaird Head')

Fraserburgh was founded in 1546 by Sir Alexander Fraser, ancestor of the Saltoun family, and the restored remains of his squat tower can still be seen on Kinnaird Head to the north of the town, surmounted by the lighthouse. Near it stands the 'Wine Tower', the origins of which are obscure, though some claim that it was from this tower that the town got its local name 'The Broch':
'Fraserburgh will be a broch
When a' the ither brochs are doon.'
Originally the town was called Philorth, and in 1592 Sir Alexander Fraser obtained a charter for the foundation of a university there: building began, but the scheme fell through and the only time it was used as a university was in 1647 when King's College moved there for a time, while plague struck Aberdeen.

Fraserburgh

The first fishing from Fraserburgh was done from the village of Broadsea — formerly Seatown — a quarter of a mile west of Kinnaird Head lighthouse and it was only in the late 18th century that boats began to fish from Fraserburgh itself. At that time there was no quay or pier there and the boats were beached at high water and allowed to lean on their sides, so that the men and women could shake the herring from the nets and take out what was in the hold. The fish were then carted away by the curers.

The 'Old Harbour' was built between 1814 and 1832 and consists of the north and south piers. In 1840 the first part of the Balaclava Harbour was constructed to the north of this, and its breakwater was lengthened in 1875 and again in 1910.

Fraserburgh

Common surnames in
Fraserburgh—
Duthie,Stephen, Tait,
Watt, Crawford, Noble,
McLennan and Taylor.

The southern breakwater was begun in 1897 making a harbour of the interconnected basins. It was only between the 1840s and the end of the last century that the town came into its own, but it grew and prospered like no other place in Scotland apart from Peterhead, with fleets of boats from the west coast and even France swelling the local fleet during the summer months. In 1855 there were 84 vessels based there, including 44 large drifters of over 30 feet in length: by 1881 the fleet had increased to 152 boats and by 1900 there was a substantial number of steam drifters.

Fraserburgh still has several major fish curing establishments (the first was built here in 1810) and today there is a sizeable fleet of seine-netters and light trawlers, as well as a number of large purse-netters which travel all round the British isles in pursuit of mackerel and herring, when EEC legislation allows.

The growth of Fraserburgh signalled the decline of the small fishing villages of Broadsea, Sandhaven, Pitulie and Rosehearty.

Sandhaven and **Pitulie** are adjacent, not unlike Inverallochy and Cairnbulg further south, and once formed a thriving port, with fish curing and boat-building yards there as well as a large stone harbour, built in 1830. With both inner and outer basins, the harbour is bigger than many other east coast ports — even important ports — and although the breakwater has been damaged in one place, it still provides shelter for half a dozen small lobster boats. Adjacent to the quayside is J. & G. Forbes & Co., Boat-builders, still successfully making fine wooden fishing boats.

Pitulie village is a perfect example of a Buchan fishing hamlet, unspoilt by modernisation or over-restoration.

During the herring boom there was fierce rivalry between the Fraserburgh fishermen and those at Buckie. Each had their own way of doing things and introduced 'technical' innovations to get the edge on their rivals. For example, the Buckie fishermen used to breed dogs especially for their skins, which they made buoys out of: the Fraserburgh men used bullocks' bladders for the same purpose.

Sandhaven

56

Rosehearty

Buchan as described by Alexander Hepburn, 1721: 'Every parish hath one fisher town at least, and many of them have two. The seas abound with fishes, such as killing, lering, codfish small and great; turbet, scate, mackrell, haddocks, whitings, flooks, seadogs and seacatts, herrings, seaths, podlars, gandues, lobsters, partens and several others. . . . There is no fishing round the island as have in our Buthquhan Coast.'

Rosehearty was founded in the 14th century, traditionally by a colony of Danes. The town was made a burgh in 1681, and in the 1850s showed signs of rivalling Fraserburgh as the chief herring port of the north-east, with 88 boats working out of there. There were 12 curing establishments and two harbours and in March the Rosehearty fleet would sail to the west coast, to fish off Coll and Tiree for cod and ling.

The well-protected harbour has a very narrow mouth, which makes it only usable by small boats today. A small swimming pool has been created close to the pierhead, and the harbour provides a base for a number of salmon cobles. Rosehearty has a small museum containing much interesting material relating to the town's history as a fishing centre.

Between Fraserburgh and Rosehearty the shoreline is low, with flat reefs running out to sea: beyond here it becomes more rugged, until it climbs to steep red cliffs, 400 feet high in places, topped by fields which slope towards the sea. Stone walls separate field from field and the countryside is altogether different from that which has gone before.

Red sandstone forms the building material for the charming village of **Pennan** — of which Peter Anson says: 'Of all the fishing villages on the east coast of Scotland Pennan must, I think, come first for picturesque situation.'

Squashed in against high crimson cliffs, the village clings to a ledge at the foot of a narrow glen, before the sandy beach runs down to the sea. Approached by road, there is no sign of habitation until the last minute, and when the village comes into view the effect is quite startling since its appearance is unlike anything in Scotland — more like a Devonshire harbour. It was one of the locations used by David Puttnam in shooting the film *Local Hero*.

There is still a small number of boats based there, fishing mainly for lobsters and crabs and a limited amount of white fish on hand lines, although most of the inhabitants of the fishers' cottages are professional people. It is a popular place with visitors, and in days gone by was especially popular with smugglers. Quarryman's Cave nearby has a natural quay and a staple in the roof is still visible, used by the smugglers to hang their lanterns as they landed the contraband silk and liquor.

At Culliecan, on Troup Head, was discovered a natural fortification and Bronze Age habitation which has been described as the earliest industrial site in Europe. Among the many shards of pottery and other artefacts found there were discovered some beads from the Rhine region of Germany — evidence that trade was conducted with the Continent from here in 700 B.C.

The fourth and last Lord Pitsligo owned the land around Rosehearty and was well respected by his tenants. After escaping from Culloden and a wanted man, he lived for years 'an extraordinary, hunted, wandering life, sometimes hidden in the houses of his tenants, sometimes in caves — as in the cave of Cowshaven at Pennan — or under bridges'.

The hunt was dropped for a while, but ten years after Culloden, when he was approaching eighty, he narrowly escaped capture by the redcoats in the parish of Rathen, hidden in a recess behind a bed in his son's house. Lord Pitsligo died aged eighty-four on the 21st December 1792, still a free man.

Pennan

It has been said that Crovie is better preserved than any other fishing village of the same sort and size in the whole of Europe: a unique architectural survivor, and without being artifically restored.

Crovie

Like Pennan, the 40 cottages of **Crovie** (pronounced 'Crivie') cling picturesquely to the foot of steep cliffs, with insufficient space between rock and sea for even back gardens or main streets. Some present their gable-ends to the sea and the others bury into the cliffside, 'like a brood of young sea-fowl nestling with their heads under their dams', as the writer of the New Statistical Account (1845) put it.

Because of its inaccessibility — even to the extent of villagers having to leave their cars either on top of the steep hill leading down to it or at one end of the village, there being no main street, Crovie has remained largely unaffected by the passing of the decades. The buildings are unchanged in any respect from what they were a hundred years ago, and even in 1884 the hamlet was considered to be 'antique' and architecturally interesting.

'Gamrie', as **Gardenstown** is known, was founded by Alexander Garden of Troup in 1720 and today the houses pile up the steep hill above the harbour in narrow terraces, built by successive generations as the fishing prospered and crowned today by the newest homes of fishing skippers.

Common surnames in:
Gardenstown—
Nicol, Wiseman, West, Watt.
Macduff—
Mackay, Paterson, Falconer, Thomson, West, Watts.
Banff—Wood.
Whitehills—
Lovie, Watson, Adamson, Findlay, Richie.

At the top of the hill above Gardenstown is one of the oldest churchyards in Scotland.

Folk memory at Gardenstown recalls that the town was first founded by people of the name Johnson who were 'fleeing from the battle'. In Gaelic Johnson—MacIan: the branch of Clan Donald who endured the massacre of Glencoe.

Many seabirds are familiar on this stretch of coatline — including the kittiwake ('kitty'), razorbill, auk ('coulter'), guillemot ('queet'), puffin ('Tammy Norie') and cormorant.

Here the town's social fabric remains as unaltered as the buildings of Crovie: still the principal activity of the town is fishing, still the majority of the people are devout Plymouth Brethren, still the inhabitants maintain a singular independence. So interesting is the sociology of Gardenstown that the University of Virginia recently completed a massive and detailed study of the town.

The survival of Gardenstown as a fishing village, and indeed its continued success, is a mystery. Its situation is inaccessible and its harbour, though good, is tidal: one might have expected the fishing to follow the same pattern as that in so many similar villages on the east coast, going into decline just before the First World War and never recovering afterwards. Not so at Gardenstown. In the 1920s there were 253 fishermen living there, and a fleet of 18 steam drifters and 30 other boats were owned by its inhabitants, the larger boats fishing out of bigger ports further along the coast. Today the town still has its own boat-building yard; the harbour was dredged in 1984; there is a fleet of about a dozen boats based there; and the town sends its menfolk to fish from harbours all over the country.

High cliffs form the coastline for the five miles between Gamrie Head and **Macduff**. This village was formerly called Doune, after the small hill which rises from its centre topped by a church, and it was not until 1783 that its name was changed, in honour of James Duff, second Earl of Fife, who built much of the town that we see today.

The town was planned around its harbour, one of the best on the Moray Firth, and comprises four separate basins — North, South, West and Princess Royal. The latter was opened in 1921, and in 1966 extensive improvements were made

Gardenstown

Macduff

to the older parts of the harbour. In addition there is an excellent slipway, capable of handling large boats; a boat-building yard owned by successive generations of the Watt family, a thriving new fish market and a customs and excise building.

The herring fishing was started at Macduff in 1815, and between 1830 and 1860 the port developed with great rapidity, more than three-quarters of the catch being cured there and exported direct to the Baltic. During the herring boom the town thrived, but unlike many other fishing ports success continued after the Great War. Macduff was one of the first ports to move over to motorised boats and eagerly adopted the Danish seine-net when it was introduced in 1921.

In 1770 at Tarlair, was discovered the renowned Well of Tarlair, a mineral spring to which visitors flocked from far and near, and which was partly responsible for the rise of Macduff. On a Sunday morning scores of tradesmen and shopkeepers in their 'Sunday best' went down to the shore and drank quantities of sea water from stone jugs and crystal tumblers, deemed to have excellent purgative qualities.

After having partaken of the salt water, a brisk walk was taken to Tarlair, where quantities of mineral water were drunk, and, 'fortified by the salt and mineral water, these health-seekers were able to defy the ennervating effects of the long, hot summers'.

Unfortunately, a wartime mine, washed in on the tide, destroyed everything.

Macduff is invariably associated with the royal burgh of **Banff**, which faces it a mile away across the Deveron Estuary and Banff Bay, and there used to be strong rivalry between the two towns — the former go-ahead and modern in attitude, the latter an old, dignified county town.

Banff's first charter was granted in 1163 by Malcolm IV and it was created a royal burgh by Robert the Bruce in 1324.

Throughout the 16th, 17th and 18th centuries it was popular with local landed gentry, many of whom had fine town houses there and deserted their draughty castles to winter in the companionable surroundings of the town. The exertions of the Banff Preservation Society have made sure that many of these old buildings have been restored, and the town today has a wonderful atmosphere of faded gentility.

Banff's customs accounts go back to 1390 and in the Middle Ages a thriving trade in hides, wool, sheepskins and salted salmon was conducted with the Low Countries. Until the early 19th century a fleet of tall ships travelled from Banff as far as the Mediterranean and the Baltic, and the smuggling associated with the town's foreign connection was so successful that the Council minutes of 1744 record that many 'fatal consequences attended this pernicious and unlawful trade'.

The handsome Fife Arms Hotel is built on the site of the ancient Black Bull Inn in Banff. The Black Bull was a famous place — although the ever-critical Dr Johnson described it as 'indifferent' — and was the scene of a murder in 1771 of a local gentleman by a military officer over one of the serving maids, for which the officer was never tried.

e old churchyard in e centre of Banff is ly about half an acre extent, yet it holds ,000 bodies, many of em those of children led by plague and ohus.

Macpherson's Rant

James Macpherson was the son of a Banffshire laird and a gypsy. He was a freebooter, a great fiddler and a man of immense strength, and at the end of the 17th century the counties of Aberdeen, Banff and Moray went in fear of him and his gypsy followers.

Finally he was caught and sentenced to death at Banff in November 1700. while awaiting execution he wrote a song, beginning 'I have spent my life in rioting', which he played to the assembled mob under the gallows in the Town Square, and then smashed his fiddle in pieces.

Robert Burns rewrote the song, to the same tune, and entitled it 'Macpherson's Rant': his version begins 'Farewell ye dungeons dark and strong'.

Lord Byron lived in Banff periodically between 1790 and 1798, and was closely connected on his mother's side to several families in the district. There are variations in the published accounts of Byron and his family history, and the legends that still float about Banff concerning his boyish escapades.

The Bombing of Banff

Duff House, close to the Bridge of Banff, was used as a POW camp for German prisoners during World War II. On one occasion it was bombed, and after the war a very large bomb, sufficient to destroy the entire building, was found, unexploded, beneath it.

Another bombing raid in 1943 destroyed the distillery and people still remember how a small burn nearby ran with whisky. Every bottle and container that could be found was pressed into service by the locals to save the precious spirit, and even horses and cows in neighbouring pastures became drunk.

Knock Head is traditionally the place where grey rats first entered Scotland, having swam ashore from a wreck on the ridge of off-lying rocks known as White Stones.

As well as trade, Banff was a successful fishing port: in 1822 there were 90 boats pursuing the herring from here, and in 1838 the New Statistical Account (1845) records that 30,000 barrels of fish were cured there annually, about half of them being exported to Germany and the rest to the West Indies and Ireland, via London and Liverpool.

Then, in the middle of the last century, the River Deveron changed its course and the harbour silted up. The larger, foreign-going ships could no longer use the port and many of the fishing boats moved to Macduff. Today several of its warehouses are still in use, and there is a boat-builder's yard in the town. The town is still a port of registration (BF), although its boats fish from other ports — mainly Macduff — and the harbour is used principally by yachtsmen.

Banff

Until 1900 when the present harbour was built behind the west side of Knock Head, **Whitehills** had no more than a rough pier quarried out of the rocks and useless in strong winds. In spite of this for many years this little harbour sheltered a sizeable fleet of fishing boats: 25 between 1830 and 1850, 150 in 1855, 158 in 1880, and in 1929 'one steam drifter, twenty-eight large motor boats of thirty feet keel and over, twenty-eight smaller boats and seven small boats'.

The place has the appearance of a typical northeast fishing village, crowded with clean stone cottages presenting their gable-ends to the sea. There has been a fair amount of modern building also, though the contemporary feel of the place belies the age of some of its cottages, let alone the fact that many of its families have lived there for over 300 years.

Peter Anson remarks that the fisherfolk of Whitehills were very up-to-date and cites as evidence the fact that in 1929 the town hall had two motor vans to sell its fish direct, rather than

The writer of the New Statistical Account (1845) remarks that the people of Whitehills differed from the majority of their countryfolk by their clear, fair complexion, and by the 'superior comeliness of the females'. The womenfolk had to perform all the usual duties of baiting the lines, preparing the fish and carrying it to market and they were '. . . allowed an influence which in any other condition of life would appear little consistent with either feminine proprietry or domestic order. (The women) . . . usually claim the entire proceeds of the white fishing, which lasts ten months of the year, as their exclusive prerogative.'

He goes on to say that the people of Whitehills were cleanly in their habits, and in consequence the 'fish cured by them has a superior reputation'.

Whitehills

going through dealers.

Today there is a fleet of 18 boats over 30 feet in length based at Whitehills, although some of them land their catches at other ports; there is also a handful of lobster boats, five fish merchants and a regular fish market. The fleet of vans from Whitehills has grown, and haddock, whiting, cod (in winter) and plaice from the village is renowned throughout the North-east. Anson went on to contrast **Portsoy** with Whitehills: 'Of all the ports on the south side of the Moray firth, Portsoy strikes the visitor as being perhaps the most derelict.'

The reason for this was the number of abandoned and ruinous warehouses that stood about the harbour: today these have been tastefully restored and converted into a pottery and a craft workshop producing objects and ornaments in 'Portsoy marble' — a soft green serpentine. Indeed so well has Portsoy been restored that it won Civic Trust and Saltire Society awards.

The first harbour at Portsoy was build by Sir Patrick Ogilvie of Boyne in the 16th century and was considered to be the safest on the north-east coast of Scotland. A lively trade with the Continent and England grew up, and indications of the town's prosperity can still be seen in the many excellent vernacular buildings in the town, including the warehouses mentioned above. Because Portsoy is older than many of the fishing villages in the area it is not so rigorously laid out; it has great charm and elegance.

A new harbour was built by the Earl of Seafield in 1825-28 but a storm swept it away and by the time it was reconstructed in 1884 the days of

Portsoy

small trading ports were at an end, and competition with Macduff and Buckie was too much. During the 1850s there were over 50 boats working at the herring from Portsoy and the harbour is still used by a few lobster and crab boats. There is one fish merchant processing fish there, but no fish is landed.

Portsoy is probably best known for its marble, a handsome green or pink serpentine, long appreciated for its beauty — indeed Portsoy provided two chimney pieces for Louis XIV's Palace of Versailles. Craftsmen still work it on a modest scale, and paperweights, chessmen and other small objects can still be obtained locally.

The last village in Banffshire is **Sandend**, once reckoned to be the most unspoilt place on the Moray Firth, and still today attractively cheerful, though a caravan park and a number of new buildings have sprung up on the edge of the village. Built on a narrow strip or 'berch' of land between the sea and brae, with its streets running at right angles to the beach and presenting their gable-ends to the sea; with its curing sheds and smoke-houses; and with its tiny harbour, Sandend is a classic North-east fishing village.

The smallness of its harbour, and the fact that during easterly gales the seas roll in across Sandend Bay and crash over the breakwater, has prevented Sandend becoming as successful as, say, Whitehills, but there is a long tradition of fishing in the community; many of the men still fish (mainly from Buckie); there are still a couple of small lobster boats using the place as a home port. There are also four fish merchants based there, and the white beaches to the east of the village are justly famous.

Sandend

THE BOATIE ROWS or
THE SONG OF THE FISHERMAN'S WIFE
*(said to have been written by a Mr Ewan of Aberdeen
who died in 1821)*

O weell may the Boatie row,
  And better may she speed;
O weell may the Boatie row,
  That brings the bairns' breid:

The Boatie rows, the Boatie rows,
  The Boatie rows fu' weell;
And muckle gude befa' the Haik,
  The Marline and the Creel.

★ ★ ★ ★ ★ ★ ★ ★

There's wee bit Johnnie scarce can speak,
  Or mint his father's name;
And yet ye'll hear him gabbing ow'r
  That daddy is come hame.

    Chorus

The pat it simmers in the low,
  The fire it bleezes fine;
And a' the smilin' faces round
  They welcome to his dine.

    Chorus

Then saftly comes the e'enin' rest,
  And bright the mornin' daw';
Syne up the nets — push aff the boat —
  A cheer — and then awa'.

    Chorus

The fair befa' the bonny Boat,
  And fari befa' the Oar;
And fair befa' the Master o't,
  Afloat or on the shore.

Chorus

MORAY
AND NAIRN

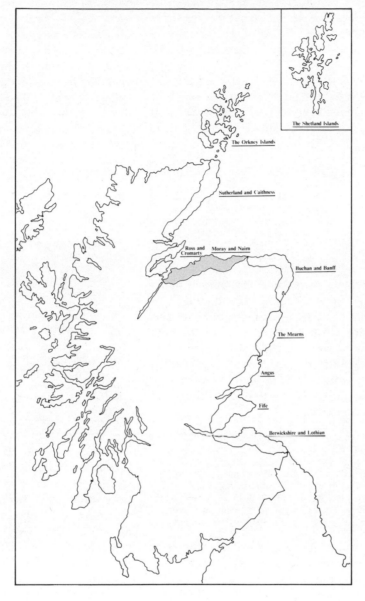

The Shetland Islands

The Orkney Islands

Sutherland and Caithness

Ross and
Cromarty

Moray and Nairn

Buchan and Banff

The Mearns

Angus

Fife

Berwickshire and Lothian

Small communities fishing for haddock, cod and ling have dotted the coast of the Moray Firth from a very early date, a few men and a handful of boats working out of every bay and creek. Local landowners made crofts and cottages available and provided grants of money with which to buy boats and gear — exacting in return a share of the catch. Sometimes the share required in 'interest' was disproportionate to the hard toil, even servitude, endured by the fishermen.

Then, in the early years of the last century, the arrival in the Moray Firth of the silver shoals of herring changed everything. At last the fishers had an opportunity to amass capital of their own.

> The Moray Firth is burning, from Fraserburgh along the whole South Coast, Macduff, Banff, Buckie, Lossiemouth, Brochhead and a score of villages besides. We've got to go ahead. No half measures now. The money will be flowing like the river. As one man said in Wick: the creels of silver herring will turn into silver crowns.
>
> **Neil Gunn,** *The Silver Darlings*

Local fishermen were joined by other seamen from distant ports; curers offered money in advance for the purchase of bigger boats and better gear; gutting and curing yards were opened at Fraserburgh (1810), Helmsdale (1813), Macduff, Portsoy, Banff and Cullen (1815), Burghead (1817) and Lossiemouth (1819). The time had come to break with the old feudal relationships.

> It was looked upon as more than an insult to ask a fisherman, on proceeding to sea, where he was going. He would be certain that some disaster would befall him, or that he would catch no fish that day. Sometimes he would answer: 'De'il cut oot yer ill tongue!' The words 'kirk' and 'church' were taboo, and should it be necessary to refer to it — and churches were often employed as landmarks — the word 'bell-hoose' was substituted.

The district of Moray opens with six villages in the space of nine miles of rocky coastline; the first is **Cullen**, a little town tucked in against a steep brae at the easternmost end of Cullen Bay.

The Cullen fishermen believed that 'Anderson' and 'Duffus' were dangerous words to mention at sea. The former was known as 'the man who sells the coals'.

The royal burgh dates from the beginning of the 13th century and the original town was 'in the shadow' of Cullen House, the splendid seat of the Earls of Seafield. George MacDonald described it in the early 19th century: 'as irregular a gathering of small cottages as could be found on the surface of the globe. They faced every way — only by their roofs could you predict their position.'

Most of the old houses were pulled down by the laird in the 1820s: they were too close to his windows for his liking, so he built the 'model' village of New Cullen and moved the fishers in there. The harbour was built in 1817, at which time there were seven large boats fishing from it and a number of skiffs and smacks.

Cullen Skink

This soup-stew originated from Cullen; 'skink' is an old Scots word for 'soup' or 'broth'.

1 large Finnan Haddock
1 medium onion, finely chopped
Salt and pepper
1 lb potatoes
2 pints of water
½ pint of milk
2 oz butter
Parsley and single cream

Put fish, onion, water and seasoning into a large pan. Bring to the boil, cover and simmer for 20 minutes. Meanwhile, peel, boil and mash potatoes. Lift out fish, leave to cool for a minute and remove skin and bones. Strain the stock and return to pan. Add flaked fish with the butter, milk and mashed potatoes. Bring to the boil and simmer two to three minutes. Garnish and serve.

Anson gives an interesting outline of the fisherman's year in *Fishing Boats and Fisherfolk*: 'From February to May the Cullen fishermen worked on grounds in the Firth some twenty to sixty miles off, being several days at sea, returning with cod, ling and skate, which were plentiful. These were cured locally, a process which took three or four weeks. June was the month for haddock fishing. On 10th July the fishermen left Cullen for the herring fishing, being absent for at least seven weeks in their open, undecked boats. On returning home they went south to Leith or Aberdeen to sell their dry fish. Arriving back at the end of September they were occupied until the following February with the haddock lines. . . . The greater part of the haddock were smoked, the rest sold in the surrounding countryside by the fishwives or 'cadgers'. Mussels for bait had to be brought from Inverness or from Ross-shire or Sutherland.'

Today the harbour is neat and clean and provides a haven for one salmon coble and a small fleet of pleasure boats.

Portknockie was founded by emigrant fishermen from Cullen in 1677. The event is recorded in the Old Statistical Account (1793): 'About twenty years ago died Katie Slater, aged ninety-six. She recollected that she was as old as the House of Faskane, as her father had often told her that he built the first house in Portknockie in the same year in which the House of Faskane was built, and that she was brought from Cullen to it, and rocked in a fisher's scull [i.e. the basket in which the lines were carried] instead of a cradle.'

Faskane House has disappeared and the Cullen Bay Hotel stands on the site of the laird of Gordon's House. Close by on the shore is a sizeable cave, in which the laird and two other local gentlemen lived for six weeks during the 1715 Rising — apparently in some degree of comfort.

The town is made up of parallel rows of neat stone cottages, most of them Victorian. Some are quite substantial and stand witness to the success of Portknockie at the end of the 19th century. The fishermen there always had a reputation for industry and enterprise, and although any who live in the town today now work out of other harbours, during the herring boom and well into the 1930s it was the deepest harbour north of Aberdeen and one of the busiest ports on the Firth. In 1929 there was a fleet of steam drifters based there, employing 555 fishermen: today eight small boats fish full time for lobsters and crabs, and for cod with lines and light nets.

West of Portknockie the coast continues wild and rugged for a mile and a half, with several small islets lying off, then it becomes gentler as the headland is rounded into **Findochty** (pronounced 'Finnechtie').

Although a charter of 1568 mentions 'port, customs and fishing grounds' at Findochty, the village was founded in 1717, when John Ord of Findochty Castle invited 13 men and 11 boys from Fraserburgh to come and settle in houses he had built there. Their names were Flett, Campbell and Smith, and until the Second World War these remained the commonest names in Findochty: the writer of the Old Statistical Account observed that the 'fisherfolk of Findochtie were distinguished for their decency and decorum and for curing their fish, great and small, superlatively well'.

In 1855 there were 140 boats working out of Findochty, but after the turn of the century, the village began to suffer from its proximity to Buckie, and by 1928 it was possible for the *Aberdeen Press and Journal* to report old fishermen remarking: 'The young women today canna sheel or bait hooks, and th' young men couldna fit on a hook. . . .'

'Porteasy', or **Portessie** as it is known today, was founded by a local landowner in 1727 with five cottages, built for a handful of fishing families who had migrated there from Findhorn, further down the coast.

At Portessie the luminescence which sometimes played around the boat's rigging (known elsewhere as Corposant or St Elmo's fire) was referred to as 'Corvie's Aunt' or 'The Covenanter'. At Findochty it was called 'Jack's Lantern'. It was universally believed to foretell the death of one of the crew's relatives.

Portknockie

The village is a typical north-eastern fishing community, with its row of cottages at right angles to the sea. There was never a harbour here, and the boats were dragged up the beach at a spot where there was — and still is — a natural little bay. Today the village is a suburb of Buckie, but it still has a strong individuality and separate identity. It was only absorbed by the larger town in 1904 and is still mainly inhabited by fishing folk, though none of them keep their boats here.

At Portessie the fishing community would gather round a new boat and cheer as one of their number threw beer over the vessel and chanted her name. Then followed 'the boat feast' — a dinner of broth, porter and large quantities of whisky.

At both Buckie and Portessie it was believed that the sea would not become calm until the body of a drowned person had been recovered and buried.

When the sound of the sea was heard in the west at Buckie the fishermen would refer to 'The chant fae th' soans o' Spey' and would expect good weather.

Buckie was originally a group of hamlets — Ianstown, Yardie and Buckpool — the earliest building taking place at Buckpool, on the west side of the Burn of Buckie, as early as 1645. During the 18th century towns grew up on either side of the burn and the place became a sizeable fishing haven, in spite of the fact that there was no harbour.

In 1793 there were 28 large boats working out of Buckie, each manned by six men. From February to April they pursued the 'Great Fishing' — seeking cod and ling about 50 miles offshore and skate off the coast of Caithness. Ling and skate were the most valuable fish on account of the oil which could be extracted from their livers: the fish were salted in pits on the beach and then dried on flat stones. At the end of June the boats sailed for Leith, Kirkcaldy or Anstruther with their holds full of dried fish: the season's work would bring between £8–£12 to

Buckie

each man, with half that for boys. Then they would return north to begin the herring fishing off the Caithness coast, which lasted six weeks. For this they were either paid on the bounty system (£8 down 'with the usual quantity of whisky', plus 5/- 'arrival money', 2/- per week for beer and 5/- 'departure money') or engaged by curers at the rate of 10/- per barrel, 'with a bottle of whisky a day in lieu of all demands'. In a bad season the former system suited the crews better, but when the fishing was good they naturally preferred the latter.

A vivid impression of the fishers of Buckie comes down to us from the Old Statistical Account (1793) where they are described as sober, frugal and industrious; peaceable and friendly neighbours; decent and exemplary in their attendance on religion:

'No moral duty is seldomer violated by them than chastity. They go to sea as boys, at fourteen years of age, become men at eighteen and marry soon after: always the daughters of fishers. . . . The men and women of Buckie are in general remarkably stout and well shaped, many of the former above common stature; and of the latter, many are pretty and dress to advantage on holidays.'

Herring curing started at Buckie soon after the Napleonic Wars, and the first harbour was built out of timber in 1843. It was swept away by a storm and a small replacement was constructed at Buckpool in 1855. This was hopelessly inadequate, but it was not until 1877 that the present 'great refuge of shipping' was completed at a cost of £600,000 by Mr Gordon of Cluny. It is very functional and simple in design, with the harbour wall running parallel to the coast and the harbour itself divided into five basins.

Since then Buckie has gone from strength to strength. A Victorian town grew up, centred around a single long, wide street with many side streets running off it — as Peter Anson, himself a Buckie man, remarks: 'All appearances of romance are subordinated to business. But where one finds the sea, ships and seafarers, one always discovers romance, if one looks deep enough.'

> Before a fisher's marriage at Buckie in the mid-19th century, the couple were required to pledge half a guinea that no fighting or rioting would take place. If, as a result of the alcoholic celebration, there was brawling, or even bloodshed, the pledge was given to the poor; if all went well it was returned to the bridegroom the following Sunday.

During the 1880s there was an average of 150 fishing boats based there: by 1900 there were nearly 500 'Zulus' registered at Buckie and fishing right around the coast of Britain. In 1902 the first steam drifters appeared, to be embraced enthusiastically by the fishermen of Buckie. The years between then and the First World War were years of unparalleled success, and there are rows of elaborately built stone houses in the town which stand witness to the money earned by fishermen at a time when Buckie was reckoned to be the fastest growing town in Scotland, and second only to Aberdeen in importance as a fishing centre. After the war they held on to the steam trawler long after most other ports had abandoned it in favour of seine-netters, confident that the export of herring would recover. It didn't and as a result the town declined for a time and many of the boats had to be sold at a loss or broken up.

> 'Tee-names' or nicknames were used in many parts on the north-east coast, especially where so many of the fishermen had the same surname. Buckie tee-names include: 'Bosan', 'Shakes', 'Perdy', 'Dooklam', 'Bodger', 'Kander', 'Fosky', 'Bullam', 'Dozie', 'Coolin', 'Bo', 'Coup' and 'Doddle Diddle'.

'Until 1850 the Buckie fishermen went barefoot in summer. His ordinary clothes were canvas trousers, "fear-nought" coat and homespun woollen shirts and drawers.'
G. Hutcheson, 1837

Portessie

The library at Buckie incorporates a small fisheries museum and has a permanent exhibition of water-colours, with the east coast villages as their subject matter, by Peter Anson.

Today, Buckie's importance has returned. There are now a fleet of 116 boats registered there (BCK), although only about 30 use the port as a home base all year round. There are chandlers, three boatbuilders' yards — including the foremost builder of wooden boats in the country — marine engineers' workshops, ice works, a fishmarket, and the largest scampi processing factory in Scotland.

Fishermen from several surrounding villages keep their boats at Buckie, including the men from **Portgordon**, although it is only a generation ago that the large harbour was so packed with boats that you could walk its length from deck to deck.

Portgordon was planned and layed out by the Fourth Duke of Gordon in 1797 to export grain from the neighbouring farmyards, and during the early 19th century it was busier than Buckie. Its decline was signalled by Buckie's rise, and during a fierce gale in 1953 the harbour was so badly damaged that it now dries out at low tide and is used only by pleasure craft and the occasional lobster boat.

Between Portgordon and Lossiemouth the great sand dunes of Spey Bar stretch for almost ten miles in a north-westerly direction, a popular place with hand-line fishermen in the district. Inland, the countryside changes subtly, with forests of Scots pine and broadleaved trees breaking up the rolling countryside, and in the distance the shadows of great mountains in the estuary of the river Spey itself, about four miles from Buckie, the country is absolutely flat and at the mouth of the river are three somewhat unusual villages. The first is **Spey Bay**, standing right on the edge of the dunes on the eastern bank. There was once a community of fishers living here, but today the cottages are holiday homes, with an excellent links golf course, a hotel and a caravan site close by. The shore is notable for its immense banks of shingle, continually being moved westwards along the coast by the drift of the sea. Three times this century — the last time in 1962 — the mouth of the River Spey has come close to being blocked by shingle and a new channel has had to be cut through.

From the long spit at the very mouth of the river — a place called 'Tugnet' — salmon fishing has been carried on for centuries, a huge ice-house was built there in 1830 to store ice for packing the fish. Today this holds an exhibition devoted to the history of the fishery, and in front of it are three restored salmon cobles.

Across the Spey are Garmouth and Kingston — only a couple of hundred yards away as the crow

flies (or on foot via the railway bridge), but nearly eight miles by road.

Ham and Haddie

A smoked haddock
Thin slices of smoked ham
Pepper

The pale, lightly smoked Moray Firth haddock is ideal for this dish. Skin a good-sized fish and cut into neat pieces. Fry the hame, set aside and keep hot while frying the fish in the ham fat. Add a little butter if required, and turn over once. Season with pepper, and arrange the ham around the fish.

Garmouth was founded in the 16th century as a port from which to export timber from the forests of Strathspey and Benmore, the trees being floated down river in great rafts. Then, in the 18th century, the fickle Spey changed direction and left the thriving port high and dry. The place has altered little from the description of it given in an early guidebook: 'The streets are nearly as sinuous as the houses, which, as regards size and position are nearly as irregular as it is possible to make them.'

Kingston, by contrast, was founded only in 1784 by a small group of English shipwrights from Kingston-on-Hull. It was laid out with long parallel streets of low-browed cottages, and its inhabitants made their living building ships out of the same timber that Garmouth had previously exported.

It is hard to imagine, today, that in the place of the acres of stones and pebbles brought down by the Spey in spate were once great shipyards, responsible for the construction of hundreds of sailing ships, some of them famous clippers.

Lossiemouth, seven miles from the mouth of the Spey is, like Buckie, a collection of formerly separate villages. The old seatown of Lossiemouth, around the original harbour, was

It was a common marriage custom in all the Moray villages for the bride and bridegroom to invite their guests by personal calls. The older folk were also invited to what was called the 'bueking', i.e. a supper which was held on an evening before the wedding when the presents were on show.

Burghead

Common surnames in Lossiemouth—Stewart, Campbell, Souter, Flett, Gault, Hay. Hopeman—Main, Sutherland, More, McPherson, Young.

James Ramsay Macdonald, Britain's first Socialist Prime Minister, was born in a fisherman's cottage at Lossiemouth, and spent his boyhood in the old 'fishertown'.

The minister writing the entry for Lossiemouth in the Old Statistical Account (1792) was clearly delighted to report that there was 'no lawyer, writer, attorney, physician, surgeon, apothecary, negro, Jew, gipsy, Englishman, Irishman, foreigner of any description, nor family of any religious sect or denomination except the Established Church' in the district.

the port for Elgin, and was founded in 1698; the residential suburbs a mile to the west, are the former fishing hamlets of Stotfield and Covesea, and founded in 1830 with the building of the 'New Harbour' is the planned village of Branderburgh. The New Harbour was cut out of solid rock to avoid the silting up which the Old Harbour was subject to at the mouth of the River Lossie. The quarried stone was used to construct the break-water which protects the outer basin from the north-west.

> The parish church of St Gerardine is named after Gernadius, a Celtic missionary who came to teach Christianity to the Picts, and lived in a 12-foot square cave. There he used to keep a light burning on winter nights to guide local fishermen in over the treacherous sandbanks. They loved him and called him the 'Holy Man'; Haliman Point is named after him, and he also appears on the town seal.

> In 1670 the fishermen of Stotfield were cited before the Kirk Session of Kinnedar for the 'idolatrous custom of carrying lighted torches round their boats on New Year's Even' and again on 18th September that same year were 'warned against going to the superstitious place called the chapel of Grace'.

In the 18th and early 19th centuries a handful of small boats fished for cod, skate, halibut, haddock, whiting and saithe, then, in 1819, the herring arrived in the Moray Firth: within 20 years the fleet grew to 45 boats, almost half of which were designed for fishing herring. Fishwives from Lossiemouth took the catches to Elgin. The port was given a tremendous boost in the 1890s after the first 'Zulu' fishing boat was built there in 1879 — named after the colonial war which was success-fully completed the same year.

The boat design combined the best elements of the 'Fifie' (the straight stem, which gave a good grip on the water shile sailing to windward) and the 'Scaffie' (the sharply raked stern, which made for

speed by increasing the waterline length and allowed more working space on the after-deck). Tradition has it that the combined design was evolved to seal a marriage agreement between two boatbuilders, each of whom specialised in the different types. The boat was named *Nonesuch* — for it was neither one type nor the other. To it was added a massive free-standing main mast, made of Norwegian whitewood and trimmed down from a baulk of timber 60 feet long and two feet square. The absence of standing rigging was a considerable advantage: there was little to entangle the gear when fishing or to become caught up with neighbouring boats when packed in harbour. Within four years of the launching of the *Nonesuch* there were 3,665 Zulus registered in Scotland, ranging from 20 feet to 80 feet in length. Lossiemouth was also the first port in Scotland to adopt the Danish seine-net method of trawling. This happened in 1921, after a disastrous herring season due to a coal strike. Tradition has it that local fishermen had been baffled the year before to see and English trawler, the *Brash*, sailing round in wide circles. They had nicknamed the boat *The Lemon Man*, and only learned what he was up to when they sailed to the English herring fishing the next year. Immediately they arrived in Grimsby the Lossiemouth skippers realised the signifi-cance of the new method and six boats abandoned the English season there and then, racing home to convert their boats to seine-netters.

Within a decade most of the boats fishing from Lossiemouth had gone over to the new method of fishing. John Campbell, a local boatbuilder, designed the first modern seine-net fishing boat, incorporating Scandinavian principles. Today Lossiemouth has a fleet of 11 light trawlers and four seine-netters fishing regularly from the harbour and landing prawns and white fish respectively for the daily market.

THE REASON WHY?

I met a herring fisherman,
    And said, Pray, state the reason
Why operations on this coast
    Have failed throughout this season?
There passed a shadow o'er his brow;
    His voice was like a tear,
As he replied—I am convinced
    The water's been too clear.

I met a herring fisherman
    Of scientific bent,
Who fruitless search, both East and West,
    Had in his drifter spent.
Of temp'ratures and currents he
    His knowledge did uphold,
And summed it up in the remark—
    The water's been too cold.

I met a herring fisherman
    For whom there was no dole,
He had not grossed much more than pay
    His black squad and his coal.
He said—The seabed was disturbed
    By yon 'quake in the spring;
And that's the cause—I'm sure of it—
    Yes, sure as anything.

I met a herring fisherman
    Net-mending at Braeheads;
He told me that sea-monsters had
    Nigh torn his gear to shreds:
He said—The grounds infested are
    With sharks of mighty daring,
Mackerel, Inkfish, dogfish, too—
    That's why there is no herring.

I met a herring fisherman—
    A leader of his class,
Who many weeks had feared
    What now has come to pass.
You want to know the cause, said he;
    I'll tell you straight and square;
We did not catch the fish, my friend
    Because—*They were not there!*

W. R. Melvin (1931)

The coastline between Lossiemouth and **Hopeman** is made up of sandstone cliffs, and the harbour of Hopeman was built to export this golden-coloured stone from the quarries at Granbrae and Clasach. Hopeman freestone has been much used for hydro-electric power stations in the Highlands. Although the town was only laid out in 1805 by William Young of Inverugie, it is likely that there was a fishing community there long before that, indeed the first fishers to settle there are supposed to have come from Ardersier. That the district was inhabited from very early times is testified to by the famous caves at nearby Covesea, the roofs of which are decorated with Pictish carvings.

Hopeman itself is attractively spare and compact in appearance, its streets sloping down to the sea and laid out at right angles to one another. Although there are still a number of fishing families living in the town, they work out of other ports and the only boats using the harbour today are pleasure craft. At its peak, in the 1880s, there were 120 boats working from here.

> On Old Year's Night, the 11th/12th January of each year, a blazing tar-barrel is paraded through the streets of Burghead and then placed in a special stone on Dowie Hill. this is known as 'The Burning of the Clavie' and is done to ward off evil spirits in the New Year, a custom that harks back to Pictish or Norse times, or even earlier, to fire-worship.

The origins of **Burghead** stretch into the dawn of time. Its name refers to the 'borg' or fortress of a Norse Yarl, Sigurd of Orkney, which was established here in 889, but even before this it was a significant place for the Picts. On the strategic headland at the end of the town is a large vitrified fort, long supposed to be Roman in origin now recognised as having been built in the Iron Age.

Burghead village is built on a narrow rock peninsula, thrusting out for half a mile into the Moray Firth. Fishing has always been the principal pursuit of the inhabitants, initially from the beach and a small pier which collapsed in the 1790s and then from the enlarged early 19th-century harbour.

A commentator in the 1840s remarked that in spite of the best possible facilities and a harbour which could be used in any wind, there was still room for many more boats than the 43 that were based there: 'There is a long range of curing yards, constructed with every attention to convenience, and each house having its smoking house, salt cellar, storehouse, gutting and packing sheds and every other necessary appendage.' There were, furthermore, regular steamers from Inverness to London and Leith calling there on every voyage.

The number of boats working from Burghead remained constant until the end of the century, and the place was now slow to embrace steam and motor-driven craft — in 1928 there were 23 steam drifters and 13 motorboats based there. Still today it is a busy little haven, with a dozen boats working from there are the height of the season and a certain amount of coastal trade, mainly associated with Morayshire's distilleries. The town has eight boats of its own, but these are work out of other ports. Above the harbour is a substantial coastguard station, built in 1807.

Findhorn

The present village of **Findhorn** is the third of that name to have been built in this vicinity. It was erected in 1701, its predecessor, which was a mile and a half north, having been swamped by the sea and the first hamlet having been buried under the shifting Culbin Sands of the estuary, some of which are over 90 feet high.

It was most important to the fisherfolk on this part of the coast that blood should be shed on Christmas morning; some of the more old-fashioned people even killed a sheep as a sort of sacrifice.

Seaweed Soup

The rejuvenating effects of the iron and iodine contained in seaweed are legendary in places like Buckie and Ullapool on the west coast: 'a dulsie man's niver oot o' bairns'.

½ lb sloke/dule/carrigeen
3 pints milk
½ lb mashed potatoes
Salt and pepper
1 oz butter
2 tablespoons lemon juice

Place seaweed, milk, potato into a pan. Boil. Simmer for 20 to 30 minutes, then liquidise or sieve or simply beat vigorously till smooth. Return to pan, season to taste and add butter and lemon juice. Bring back to boil, then allow to simmer for a few minutes before serving. Serves six to eight. (Dried seaweed may also be used.)

A present of fish on New Year's Day was an omen of good fortune. It was unlucky if the first person one saw on New Year's Day was of dark complexion, but lucky if he was fair.

In the 17th century Findhorn was the principal port in Moray, having been set up by local lairds engaged in trade with the Continent. Wines, silks, tapestries and other luxuries were imported, and beef, hides, salmon, grain and malt exported.

Fishing was also conducted from there, but such was the gentry's control of the harbour that it was a fixed rule that: 'All such skate, ling, etc., as shall happen to be slain and landed at the town and port of Findhorn' must remain in the boats for the space of 24 hours, during which time the citizens of Forres and the country gentlemen of the district had the opportunity of buying what they wanted, at a fair price. Any skipper who sold his fish 'to the great prejudice of the town and county' suffered heavy fines: in 1636 four fishermen were fined £100 for this offence.

In the larger fishing boats of the middle of the last century, the crew usually consisted of eight men, each of whom had their distinctive name. Those in the bow are known as 'harksmen'. At a feast — a 'boat feast' — all sat together as they would at sea. Drinking was often carried on throughout the night. A common toast was:
'Health t' men, an' death t' fish,
They're wagging their tails, it'll pay for this.'

In spite of its former celebrity as a trading port, there has never been a proper harbour at Findhorn — security is gained from the sheltered waters of Findhorn Bay and from two small stone piers and the quay itself. However, the difficulty that boats encountered in getting over the sand-bar at the mouth of the bay when the wind was in the north may have discouraged fishing from there: even during the herring boom there was only a small fishing fleet working out of Findhorn. There is no commercial fishing done from the harbour today, though the place is a popular yachting centre, and has a yacht club with Royal status. There is also a salmon station there. A group of ancient, semi-subterranean ice-houses are still in use to the north of the village.

Mavistoun Gouks

'A few miles east of the town of Nairn there existed till almost eighty years ago a little fishing village called Mavistoun. The Boetian simplicity of its inhabitants is to this day a byword. "The fisher-gouks of Mavistoun" is a line that occurs in a poem by a now forgotten local bard. If a tithe of the stories still current among the Nairn fishermen about them have any foundation in fact, they were the most superstitious, the most ignorant and lazy of their kind. At the trial of the famous witches of Auldearn one of the women confessed that whenever they wanted fish they had only to go to mavistoun and repeated the following incantation:
The fishers are gane to the sea,
And they'll bring hame fish to me;
They'll bring hame intil the boat,
But they'll get nane o' the smaller sort
to get from the terrified fishermen as many as they wanted.

It is said that once a fisherman found a horseshoe on the beach. It was the first that had ever been seen, and all the wise men in the little community gathered together to examine it. One of them at last hazarded the opinion that it was a bit of the moon — in fact, a new moon. This view was promptly contradicted by the man, who being the oldest, was regarded as the wisest among them. "A moon it was," he believed; "but it could not be a new moon, otherwise it would be up in the sky." For himself, he had often wondered what became of the old moons. This settled it. The old moons fell to the earth and this was one of them.'
Charles G. Rampini, *History of Moray and Nairn,* **1897**

The once populous fishing village of **Mavistown** is now semi-derelict — no more than a cluster of cottages. It is also about a mile from the coast, the Culbin Sands having shifted.

The fishers at Mavistown were known locally as 'fisher-gouks' and were regarded as preposterously superstitious even by their superstitious brethren.

In Nairn salmon could never be mentioned on board a boat except by the name of 'Spey codling'. A horse was referred to as the 'four-footed beast'.

It was unlucky to see a salmon leap in front of the boat; to whistle when on board, to pick up a parcel for a friend and to meet a cockerel before going to the fishing.

There were unlucky hours, days, months and seasons. It was unfortunate to be born between midnight and one in the morning, for such a child saw 'feart' things — ghosts and apparitions.

Shortly after he had ascended the throne of England in 1603, James VI and I boasted that he had a town in his northern kingdom 'sae lang that the inhabitants at one end didna understand the language spoken at the other'. The town he referred to was **Nairn**, where it is claimed that the Highland Line intersects the High Street: the folk on the north-east speaking Gaelic, those on the south-west English. The fishers are on the 'English' side of the town, though they are largely of Norse extraction. Common surnames in Nairn stand witness to this: 'Main' and 'Ralph' for example are corruptions of 'Magnus' and 'Hrolf'.

The fisher town of Nairn is very different in feeling and appearance from the rest of the town, its tiny houses crowded together haphazardly close to the River Nairn, although prosperous fishermen moved into more substantial villas to the east of the town in the early decades of this century. Today the Fishertown Museum has exhibitions and exhibits relating to the way of life of the folk there.

When Boswell and Johnson visited Nairn in 1773, and described it as 'in a state of miserable decay', they were correct. Twenty years later, the parish minister, the Rev. John Morrison, wrote in the Old Statistical Account: 'The number of people who want employment in the town and its vicinity is absolutely incredible. . . . The poor are extremely numerous and many of them very indignant indeed.'

In the 18th century a fleet of six boats sailed after white fish, having to go as far as Sutherland or Caithness waters to make their catches. By the 1850s the port was more prosperous, but still one commentator was forced to comment that:

'The port of Nairn is another of those places where it is clearly proved that there is something radically wrong in the present condition of the Scottish herring industry. There are 60 boats annually fitted out from it, yet none of these remain at home; they all seek employment at the neighbouring stations, or on the coast of Caithness. About the year 1828 there were cured at this station between 17,000 and 18,000 barrels of

herrings, and now the business is quite forsaken.'

J. Thomson, *The Scottish Fisheries*, 1849
Shortly after this was written, however, the original harbour — which had been built in 1820 by Thomas Telford — was extended, and the latter decades of the last century were years of prosperity for the Nairn fishermen: in 1882 there were 91 boats fishing from there, and the port ranked third on the Moray Firth, after Buckie and Portknockie. A new harbour was built in 1932, but by that time the industry was in decline and Nairn's heyday had passed. There are only a handful of boats fishing from the harbour today, although the sheltered basin is very popular with yachtsmen.

The fisherfolk of Nairn were almost as superstitious as those of Mavistown. For example, it was considered very unlucky to burn fishbones or the shells of bait, and there was a well-known rhyme:

> *Bile me, fry me,*
> *But dinna burn my banes,*
> *Or I'll lay scarce*
> *On your hearth stane.*

On New Year's Day the fisherfolk would walk down to the beach, fill a bottle with salt water and collect some seaweed. The water was sprinkled around the house, the seaweed put above the door, on the hearth and in the roof-beams, and all this brought good luck in the coming season.

Practices like this were loudly condemned by the Kirk, but the terrors of eternal damnation were not sufficient to suppress the old customs, nor to subdue the fishers' natural independence of character, bequeathed to them by their Scandinavian ancestors.

West of Nairn the coastline is low and wooded, then round Craigmee Point, the Inner Moray Firth is entered, protected by Fort George.

One and a half miles further on lies **Ardersier**, which means *'ard nan Saor'*, the 'headland of the carpenter'. Ardersier is also known as Campbelltown, after its original inhabitants, and in the 16th century was the site of a struggle between the Campbells of Cawdor and the Mackintoshes. The Mackintoshes did much damage to the village, 'depaupering of the tenantis and occupearis thereof and debarring of the saidis personis . . . fra any manner of fisching in that part callit the stell of the ness of Arthur-schier be braking of their coublilis and cutting of their nettis'.

The village is one of the oldest fishing ports on the Moray Firth coast and was once of some importance. It straggles along the sandy shore for over a mile and to the south some old fishers' cottages are still standing.

There was no harbour — the boats were pulled up the beach — although there was an old wooden pier, the remains of which can still be

The "Pansy"

seen. White fish, herring and salmon were all caught, and 11 boats of 12 tons register sailed to the herring fishing at Helmsdale or Burghead. During the 1880s it was not unusual for them to catch 200 cran in five or six weeks.

The fishermen of Ardersier married unusually young and their 'penny weddings' were famous. All the surrounding countryside were invited, and contributed small sums of money to pay for the privilege. After the celebration, it was customary for the bride to make a round of the neighbourhood and her friends were all obliged to present her with a piece of furniture or some other 'substantial gift'. This practice was known as 'thigging'.

Petty or Fisherton comprised the pre-Reformation parishes of Petyn and Bracholy and was for centuries a powerful thanedom, lordship and barony. In the 1880s there were almost as many boats fishing from here as from Ardersier: today the hamlet is so small that it is only marked on large-scale maps.

The village lies three miles south-west of Ardersier on a slight rise above the shore, with fine views over the Firth and to north and south. It was a famous place for smuggling contraband in and out of Inverness. Claret, brandy and silks were brought in and whisky sent out: a primitive import/export trade which is unique on this coast. Every time a shipment arrived on the beach a runner was sent to a tobacconist in the town bearing an empty snuff-box. If the coast was clear the tobacconist would fill the box full of snuff: if it was prudent to delay, he would fill it half full. In this way orders could be given even if there were excisemen in the very shop.

The Old Church of Petty behind Castle Stuart is the burial ground for many of the Chiefs of Mackintosh, and in the Bay of Petty, close by, is the famous 'Travelled Stone of Petty'. This boulder, seven feet long and six feet wide, originally served as a boundary marker, but during the hard winter of 1799 it moved 260 yards onto the frozen bay. On the night of 19th February it floated on an ice-floe to its present position.

Inverness can claim greater antiquity than almost any other town in Scotland. It was a

ctor Boece records
t there were beavers
ng on the shores of
ch Ness in the 11th
tury, and an Act of
rliament from the
gn of David I
ords 'beveris skins'
ong Scottish exports
m Inverness.

recognised capital as easily as the 6th century when Saint Columba visited the Pictish King Brude there and converted him to Christianity; it received its royal charter from David I (1124-1153) and William the Lion (1165-1214) fortified the town and granted the right to hold a weekly market.

As early as 1249 shipbuilding was an important industry at Inverness, excellent timber being available from the massive forests in the neighbourhood, and from the 13th century there was extensive trading with Europe, mainly Belgium and Holland. The principal exports were wool, cloth, hides, fur, fish and coffee, and at this time Inverness was also the principal station for the herring fishing in the Moray Firth: in 1263 it is recorded that the Sheriff of the county bought twenty 'lasts' of herrings for the King's household.

Since medieval times, however, fishing has not been an important industry at Inverness — even during the herring boom there were only a handful of boats based there. Most of the fishermen that did use Inverness as a home port came from Clachnaharry just to the west of the town, and the little village still has an unspoilt charm about it, though the main road to Beauly runs through it.

Clachnaharry was chosen to be the northern end of Telford's Caledonian Canal, the great

waterway that links the east coast with the west, and with its construction in the early 19th century Inverness became much more important as a fishing centre. Muirtown Basin, at the actual sea lock, and Loch Dochfour near the northern end of Loch Ness, provided sheltered anchorages for up to 30 steam trawlers and drifters, and many would spend the winter there. Until the First World War the town had a regular fish market and a small shipyard building steel drifters, but between the wars most of the Inverness boats moved east to Buckie, closer to the fishing grounds. No fishing is done from Inverness today, although it is still a port of registration.

Inverness has a very good local museum with a particularly interesting collection of artefacts and clothes relating to the Highland way of life.

In 1384 a large array of Islesmen advanced to Kessock Ferry and sent a message to the town, threatening to destroy it unless a large ransom was paid. The wily provost pretended to agree to the terms and sent a quantity of spirits to the chief and his fillowers who, predictably, became hopelessly drunk. The provost and citizens of Inverness than attacked them and massacred almost the entire force.

e magistrates of
verness used to post
vatchman on the
oll above Clach-
harry to look out for
ghland raiders from
e north-east.

ROSS AND CROMARTY

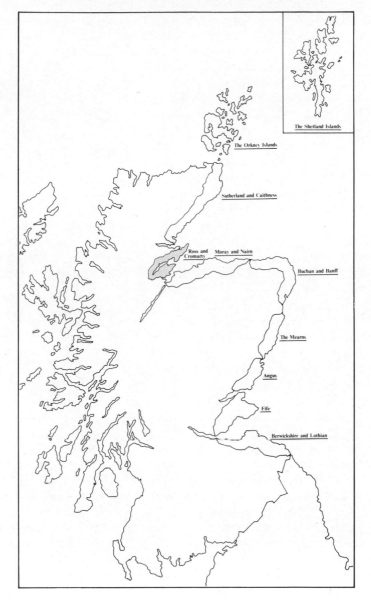

The eastern coastline of Ross and Cromarty is bounded by the Inner Moray Firth to the south and by the Dornoch Firth to the north and it is riven by the Cromarty Firth.

The first five villages in this section surround the Black Isle—so called because of the great forest of dark pines which grew there in days gone by. The land is old and fertile: the villages are sheltered by the Moray and Cromarty Firths, and many of them are of great antiquity.

The six northern villages cluster about the Tarbat peninsula, the easternmost part of the county, stretching towards the northern fishing grounds. The coastal strip behind the villages is generally rolling pasture land, but one is continually aware of the great mountain fortresses which make up the major part of the county, stretching as far as the west coast.

The first fishing village on the northern shore of the inner Moray Firth — the Inverness Firth as it used to be known — is **Avoch**, some five miles north-east of the new Kessock Bridge.

Avoch means 'field of the steam' in Gaelic; there is no evidence of either field or stream, but the village is unique on the east coast for being surrounded by trees. It stretches along a narrow coastal strip with wooded braes climbing up behind. Many of the houses present their gable-ends to the sea, and many of the street names recall the Mackenzie lairds, and their ladies, who formerly owned the village and much of the surrounding land.

There is some doubt about where the fisherfolk of Avoch originally came from, for they are certainly not of Highland origin. A persistent tradition holds that their ancestors were Spanish, arriving from a galleon wrecked during the Armada in 1588: others claim that they were Welsh or Cornish, others that their origins are Norse. Certainly their surnames are peculiar to the village — though they are scarcely Spanish sounding!

The Rev. James Smith wrote a detailed account of the lives of the fishers of Avoch in 1793 for the Statistical Account, and his observations hold true for many east coast villages, particularly as they related to the role of the women-folk.

Brought up on a diet of fish, oatmeal and potatoes, the fishers were a hardy and robust race, and the women were as strong as the men. They thought nothing of carrying a hundred pounds of fish in a creel on their backs and, since there was no pier at Avoch until 1814, would also carry their men through the surf to the boats, whatever the weather, so that their feet would remain dry for the day's fishing. Likewise they unloaded the catch and gear (the tackle for an average-sized boat might weigh three or four tons), and were responsible for gathering bait, preparing the lines and growing hemp for nets, which were made at Avoch for other fishing

Common surnames in Avoch—Patience, Jack, McLeman, Reid, Skinner.

Sir Alexander McKenzie of Avoch, the explorer of the North-West Territories of Canada, after whom the McKenzie River is named, was responsible for building the first harbour of Avoch in 1814. He died in 1820 and is buried in the parish kirk.

Avoch

stations all over the north and west of Scotland. 'Withal,' the Rev. Smith remarks, 'there were few women in the country so cleanly, healthy or so long-lived.'

The parish kirk of Avoch dates from 1670 and has a fine steeple containing one of the bells of the Fortrose Cathedral. This bell was removed from Fortrose by Oliver Cromwell, who planned to install it in his new citadel at Inverness. The bell was washed overboard, however, and was only recovered when it fouled a fishing net about a hundred years ago.

The men were at sea all week. From the beginning of October to the middle of March they sought the small herring in the upper part of the Inverness Firth, very highly regarded for their flavour, and generally fished by night; in April they sailed up to Caithness for cod, skate and haddock; in May and June some of the boats were employed by the Northumberland Fishing company to catch lobsters and crabs for the London market, taking their catches down to Newcastle once a year in their small open boats; others fished for haddock to sell locally. In mid-July the entire Avoch fleet sailed to Loch Broom or the coast of Caithness for six or eight weeks for the northern herring and ling fishing.

The 12 boats based at Avoch today all fish from west coast harbours during the season, leaving

Fisher Weddings at Avoch

The fisherfolk of Avoch married young — indeed, most men had their own houses by the age of twenty. Weddings took place on Friday afternoons, so that the whole of Saturday and Sunday could be devoted to the celebrations, and until the end of the 19th century an ancient custom was scrupulously observed 'to defy the powers of witchcraft' during the ceremony.

'When the bridegroom's party arrives at the church door, the best man unties the shoe upon the left foot of the bridegroom, and forms a cross with a nail or knife upon the right side post of the door. The shoe of course remains untied till next morning.'

(Rev. James Gibson, 1845)

behind one full-time prawn and lobster boat and a handful of part-timers. The village still has the powerful feel of a fishing community, however, with chandlers and fishermen's bars, and the 'Ochies' have a great reputation in the Black Isle. The boats used were scaffies, with an average overall length of about 30 feet, but the Avoch boats were unusual in carrying an enormous area of canvas. The main mast was as long as the boat, able to support 80 square feet of mainsail, and in addition there was a foresail about one-tenth of this size. 'Several gentlemen of the Navy have expressed their surprise at this and declared that they have seldom seen such common fishermen carry so greater proportion of sail, nor manage it more dexterously on any part of the British coasts.'

Between Avoch and Fortrose, **Chanonry Point** juts towards Fort George, creating the inner Moray Firth. Much of the Point is a golf course today, intersected by the road which runs to Chanonry Ness lighthouse and passes Ness House on the outskirts of Fortrose. This was formerly the Black Isle poor house and has now been converted into flats. Salmon fishing has long been an important industry on Chanonry Point, and an ancient ice-house stands witness to this.

Close to the lighthouse on the Ness itself is the pier from which a ferry used to leave regularly for Fort George, and nearby is a memorial cairn commemorating Coinneach Odhar, the famous Brahan Seer, who was burned as a wizard in the 16th century and whose prophecies are still coming true today.

The Brahan Seer was a retainer of the Mackenzie Earls of Seaforth and made himself very unpopular with his masters for foreseeing events which would disgrace the House of Seaforth and the whole of Scotland. He prophesied many developments in the Highlands which came

The Brahan Seer's Final Prophecy

In 1660 the Chief of Mackenzie was sent to Paris on State business. He took a long time to complete the small matter, and his wife, the Countess Isabella, asked Coinneach Odhar for news. For a long time he refused, but at last, at a gathering of the clan in the hall of Brahan Castle, he told the Countess: 'Your lord has little thought of you or his children or of his Highland home. I see him on his knees before a fair lady, his arm around her waist and her hand pressed to his lips.' For his pains, the Countess Isabella had him arrested as a sorcerer, and he was later burned in a tar barrel on Chanonry Point.

about hundreds of years later: the arrival of the railway, for example, and the building of the Caledonian Canal. He even foretold how there would come a time when the brave clansmen would flee before an army of sheep, a direct reference to the Highland Clearances.

The names of both **Fortrose** and its close neighbour **Rosemarkie** have nothing to do with horticulture: the 'rose' in each refers to 'ross', the Gaelic for 'point', and their names derive from 'Fo-tir Ros', 'the place beneath the point', and 'Rosmarcanaidh', 'the horse burn at the point'. Fortrose is the principal town of the Black Isle, and although it was created a royal burgh in the same year as Rosemarkie (1455), the latter is far more ancient. St Moluag, a follower of St Columbus and a missionary to the Picts, established a cell at Rosemarkie in the middle of the 6th century, and in 716 A.D. St Boniface built a monastery on the site. A Pictish stone in the 19th-century church is traditionally known as the gravestone of St Moluag and the site of the original abbey.

In 1124 David I founded a bishopric there and the ecclesiastical centre was moved to Fortrose, where schools of divinity and law were thrown up in the shadow of the church. The distinguished red sandstone ruins that stand witness to this important centre of learning were once a fine example of the Early Decorated style and date from the beginning of the 14th century. The abbey was destroyed by Oliver Cromwell, who transported much of the masonry to Inverness.

> There are a number of initials carved on the soft sandstone of the remains of Fortrose Cathedral — mostly the work of 17th century political prisoners. In 1880 a hoard of silver coins minted in 1100 was discovered in the cathedral green.

Fortrose's small harbour is at Chanonry, on the western side of the point and on the very edge of the town. A yacht club is based there and a number of small yachts use it as a shelter. Rosemarkie was an important salmon station, marketing the fish caught on Chanonry Point as well as those caught along the sandy beaches of Rosemarkie Bay. The ice-house at Chanonry Ness has already been remarked upon: there is another in the town at the foot of Kincurdie Drive.

So many salmon were caught here that the fish were once sold at threepence (about 1p) a pound and farm servants in the district became so tired of it that they refused to eat salmon more than twice a week.

The Faeries of Fortrose

It is said that Scotland's greatest wizard, Michael Scott, called up 'the hosts of Faery' and required them to build the cathedrals of Elgin and Fortrose. This they did in a single night, making no mistakes in the construction except that they mixed up the location of the buildings, so that the church intended for Elgin was built on the Black Isle and vice versa.

Having completed this job they returned to the wizard 'like a posse of Irish labourers thrown out of a job', clamouring for more employment. The wizard was afraid that he might be torn to pieces and saved himself by ordering them to build a causeway between the Black Isle and Ardersier.

Before midnight they had thrown up the great mound of Chanonry Point and the peninsula which now supports Fort George, but then an intoxicated Highlander came by and bade them 'God speed' in their work. This broke the spell, arrested forever the construction of the causeway and saved the navigation of Inverness.

Hugh Miller

Pioneering geologist, stonemason, author and theologian, Hugh Miller was born in Cromarty in 1802. The son of a ship's captain, Miller was apprenticed to a stonemason, and developed the phenomenal powers of observation and deduction which were to make him famous while he worked at his craft. His last work as a stonemason was the small headstone for the grave of his first child which can still be seen in the burial ground of St Regulus at Cromarty.

His thatched cottage, preserved by the National Trust, was built about 1650 by Miller's forebear John Fiddes, who was a buccaneer. The geologist once saw Fiddes' ghost, and today the cottage houses an interesting collection of fossils, manuscripts and letters.

He made his earliest geological researches in the bed of the Eathie Burn, five miles north of Rosemarkie and described the area as 'a deeply secluded dell of exquisite though savage beauty', remarking that he had spoken with an old women who claimed to have seen myriads of fairies dancing by the side of the burn when she was a girl.

On either side of the mile-wide entrance to the Cromarty Firth rise some steep hills known as the Soutors. The village of **Cromarty** clusters about a peninsula on the southern shore; neat and compact, and of considerable antiquity, guarding the entrance to the Firth which the Romans knew as *'Portus Salutis'*.

Five miles east of the Soutors, between Cromarty and Burghead, is the Guillam Bank, a shallow patch about two miles long which was once the best fishing ground in the whole Moray Firth, attracting herring boats from all over Scotland. At one time the average catch on the bank during the season was 1,000 barrels a day, and in addition to this the herring would swim right into the Cromarty Firth itself. With such an abundance of good fishing close by, the town prospered: in the 17th century there was no busier port in the entire country, and it was one of only 16 ports in the United Kingdom which required a customs clearance certificate.

Sir Thomas Urquhart, Knight of Cromarty

The preposterous figure of Sir Thomas Urquhart of Cromarty, who has been described as 'all but admirable', swaggers through the history of the English Civil War like a Falstaff. Born about 1611, Sir Thomas was a vehement writer and a passionate royalist. In his lifetime he wrote 128½ folio quires of manuscript — an *oeuvre* which he transported about with him while he was campaigning — and translated the complete works of Rabelais. He boasted that he could trace his ancestry right back to Adam, and is reputed to have died of laughter on hearing about the restoration of Charles II in 1660.

Cromarty

Common surnames in
Cromarty—Hossack,
Watson, Hogg,
Skinner, Finlayson.

A curious feature of the
dialect of Cromarty is
the habit of dropping
the 'h'—almost
unknown in Scotland,
although prevalent in
England.

Gulls are considered
lucky because they
clean up the shore and
because, as the "ocean
eagle", they show that
land is near. No one
would kill a gull
though the children
used to catch them with
baited hooks and keep
them.'

Seagull's eggs were
retrieved from the cliffs
. . . and made a
welcome addition to
their diet.'

There was never a
harbour at Shandwick;
the fishermen used the
pier at Balintore,
immediately adjacent.
In 1882 there were 45
men and boys going to
the fishing from
Shandwick in a fleet of
10 small boats.

By the end of the 18th century herring had stopped coming into the Firth, and the contributor to the Statistical Account (1793) remarked only that the fishermen were too timid to venture far out to sea. In other respects, however, the town prospered: in 1772 George Ross of Pitkene, a local laird, rebuilt the harbour, established a cloth factory, a nail and spade factory, a brewery and a lace-making works. He also built a Gaelic chapel for the Highlanders who flocked to the cloth mills. Roofless today, it still stands on a hill above the town.

> Rising abruptly above the town is a steep hill, on the summit of which formerly stood the old castle of the Urquharts, 'a massy, time-worn building, battlemented, stone-roofed and six storeys high'. It was razed to the ground in 1772 and its place taken by Cromarty House, near which stands a lifesize statue of Hugh Miller, geologist and author, by Handyside Ritchie.

Until modern times, Cromarty suffered from the continual encroachment of the sea. In late mediaeval times the town was much larger; now this part is entirely submerged and on exceptionally low tides the 'Kirk Stanes' can still be seen to the east of Fishertown; all that remains of the church and graveyard founded by St Moluag in the 6th century and long ago covered by the sea. Writers in the 19th century often remarked about the 'quaint and derelict' appearance of the town: the charm of Cromarty is largely the same today. Some of the old buildings have been well restored, and a scheme launched by the District Council and the National Trust is doing much good work in the old Fishertown (which has

been described as a gem of Scottish Vernacular architecture), but the feel of the town is one of graceful decay. There were 47 shops there before the war: today there are three, but pottery, jewellery, knitwear and woodcarving studios are thriving, and Cromarty is gaining something of a reputation as a craft centre.

Across the Firth from Cromarty is Nigg Bay, once the home of the writer Eric Linklater, now an important centre for the manufacture and repair of North Sea oil platforms and also a notable nature reserve. The largest oil rig built in the British Isles was built there in 1978 and the yard dominates the Firth with a copse of cranes. Close to the village of **Shandwick**, and right beside the road, is an ancient cross slab eight feet high, decorated with very worn figures. This cross was one of three — the others being at Nigg and at Hilton — and each is said to mark the graves of three sons of a Danish king whose ship was wrecked on the coast nearby.

The name 'Shandwick' means 'sandy bay' and the beach was much used for landing coal, lime and slates, and for loading timber and potatoes. The bay abounds in shellfish and shallow water fish, and the shore used to supply bait for many of the villages along the Moray Firth.

> 'Rabbits were freely poached on Shandwick Hill and Cadboll Cliffs, and made very good eating. The poachers sold them from door to door for 1/- to 1/6d. per pair and later from 2/6 to 3/- until the beginning of the Second World War. Scarrows (cormorants) were shot and stoned on the rocks, and then skinned and boiled for broth and eaten. They tasted just like wild duck.'

Balintore and **Hilton of Cadboll** — 'the bleaching town' and 'the hill town' — both grew up as fishing villages, with a harbour at Balintore built in the 1890s, a pier at Hilton, a boatbuilder, a sailmaker and curing yard all available to fishermen. Barrels of salt herrings went to Russia, and the harbour at Balintore also exported grain and potatoes. The harbour is still used by a handful of small boats, mainly pleasure craft, though there are some part-time lobster fishermen, and there is a salmon station in the village, with its drying green and anchors close to the harbour.

Not far from the harbour was a mound, known locally as 'Ghost's Hillock' and long regarded with superstition: anybody who passed by the place dropped a stone into a hollow to ward off the evil spirits. Quite recently the hillock was levelled to make way for new houses, and many human remains were unearthed: the place turned out to have been a Bronze Age burial ground.

Many of the inhabitants of Hilton came there after having been driven out of their homes during the Clearances. They were Gaelic speakers and members of the Free Church. The village was known locally as 'Tir Goshen' — 'the land of Goshen' — for every house was God-fearing. The three churches in the small village all attract large congregations today, and such is the enthusiasm and devotion of the people that a new Free Church was built at Hilton as recently as 1980.

A certain amount of salmon fishing is still done from the small pier and narrow, sandy beach, although it dries out at low water.

At Cadboll Point, about a mile north of Hilton, the sandy shore and low braes give way to a long line of cliffs about 150 feet high. These continue in a north-easterly direction as far as the dramatic peninsula of Tarbat Ness, some seven miles further on.

Three miles from Tarbat Ness lighthouse is the picturesque village of **Rockfield**. Little more than a row of cottages sandwiched between the rocky shore and cliffs, there is nevertheless room for tiny strips of garden behind the houses.

Rockfield was built during the herring boom in the 1880s and has a short stone pier and slipway rather than a harbour. In 1886 there were 18 boats fishing from here, providing work for 54 fishermen. There is still some salmon fishing done from here, and a couple of lobster boats regularly use the pier.

Half a mile from Rockfield are the impressive ruins of Balone Castle, still remarkably intact, although the house has not been lived in since 1650. It was originally built by the Earls of Ross and later inhabited by the Earls of Cromarty. Almost directly opposite, on the western side of the Tarbat peninsula, is the thriving village of **Portmahomack**, facing the Dornoch Firth.

The bay on which the town is situated has a sandy beach, the place is well sheltered from the chittering east wind and the views across the

Rockfield

On a low hill behind the village sits Tarbat Old Parish Church, surrounded by ancient gravestones. The church is in poor condition, although its roof and windows are still intact: it was built in 1250 and restored in 1757.

Firth to the mountains of Sutherland are impressive: it is not without good reason that Portmahomack is a popular holiday resort.

The first stone pier was built there by the Earl of Cromarty, and this was lengthened and improved by Thomas Telford, the famous harbour builder, in 1810. At the pierhead there are two fine old warehouses, one of them dating from the 17th century and still smelling of fish, and nearby is an old ice-house — all reminders of Portmahomack's former importance as a fishing port. In 1830 there were as many as a hundred boats fishing from here and six thriving curing yards engaged boats to supply them with fish all the year round. Two years later a cholera epidemic which had come from Hindustan in 1817 and swept Europe, claimed one-fifth of the population. The port is still used by two full-time lobster boats and is crowded with pleasure craft during the summer.

The small village of **Inver**, four miles south-west of Portmahomack, lost over a third of its population in the 1832 cholera epidemic and it struck with such terrifying rapidity that 11 corpses had to be buried without shroud or coffin. Many of the inhabitants fled to the hills and woods but 'the pest followed them to their hiding-places and they expired in the open air'. A certain amount of fishing was carried on from Inver — 'haddock and flounder are the staple kinds of fish; cod, whiting and skate are also found in abundance, as is herring in its season', writes the contributor to the New Statistical Account — but the place prospered principally from its extensive mussel beds, used as bait by

'Skinner' is a common name among fishermen in many of the villages of Ross-shire; Inver is also referred to as 'Inverskinnertown' in the old records.

fishermen up and down the coast.

'Pipe-smoking was common, the clay pipe, with thread wound round the stem to prevent cancer of the lip, and the briar being used, with perhaps an expensive meerschaum brought home as a present by a member of the family in the Merchant Navy. Snuff was used by the older generation, women as well as men indulging the habit.'

Most of the houses in the village today are modern bungalows, but the old fishers' cottages, much modernised, can still be seen at the eastern end of the village.

Although close to the sea, neither of the principal towns in this part of Scotland — Tain and Dornoch — have ever had any connection with fishing, and the shores of the Dornoch Firth are too far from the fishing grounds to have made worthwhile the establishing of fishing communities.

The Last Witch

The last witch to be burned in Britain was executed in Dornoch parish in 1727.

Janet Horne and her daughter were brought before Captain David Ross, deputy sheriff of the county, charged with witchcraft and consorting with the Devil on the sole ground that the unfortunate daughter was lame in both feet and paralysed in both hands. To the superstitious people of that time this meant that her mother had used her as a 'Horse and Hattock' and that the girl had been 'shod by the devil'.

The sheriff was satisfied that the charge had been proved and the unfortunate old mother was burned in a tar barrel. Her daughter escaped punishment and later married, passing her deformity to her children.

Inver

SUTHERLAND
AND CAITHNESS

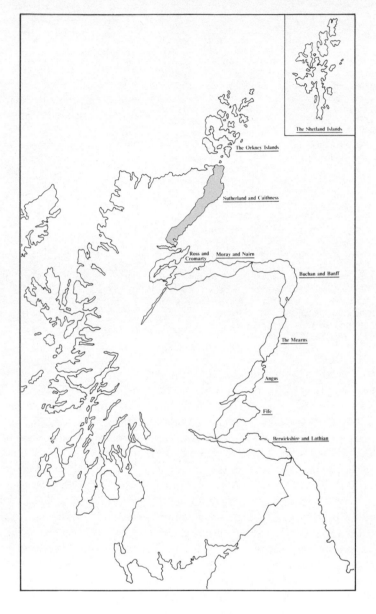

Sutherland was named by the Vikings as the land to the south of Caithness, and this is an indication of the degree to which the two northern counties of Scotland were colonised by the Norse in days gone by.

The Crofter's Home, 1807

'Their huts were of the most miserable description; they were built of turf dug from the mountainside. Their roof consisted of the same material, which was supported on a wooden frame constructed of crooked timber. . . . They (i.e. the huts) were placed lengthways, and sloping with the declination of the hill. This position was chosen in order that all the filth might flow from the habitation without further exertion on the part of the owner. Under the same roof and entering at the same door were kept all the domestic animals belonging to the establishment.

'The upper portion of the hut was appropriated to the use of the family. In the centre of this upper division was placed the fire, the smoke from which was made to circulate throughout the whole hut for the purpose of conveying heat into its furthest extremities — the effect being to cover everything with a black, glossy soot, and to produce the most evident injury to the appearance and eyesight of those most exposed to its influence.

'The floor was the bare earth, except near the fireplace, where it was rudely paved with rough stones. It was never levelled with much care, and it soon wore into every sort of inequality. Every hollow formed a receptacle for whatever fluid happened to fall near it, where it remained until absorbed by the earth. It was impossible that it could ever be swept; and when the accumulation of filth rendered the place uninhabitable, another hut was erected in the vicinity of the old one.'

(James Macdonald)

Between 1810 and 1820 the Duke of Sutherland cleared the inner part of the county of crofters, allotting to them small plots of lands near the coast or an offer of transportation to Canada. During this period most opted for the former, but few had the skills required to pursue the fishing, and by the middle of the century many of the hamlets set up were abandoned in favour of emigration. The misery and suffering endured by the expanding population, trying to survive on tiny plots of poor land, can scarcely be imagined. The original hamlet of **Embo** was one such settlement. Its site is now a caravan park and the village as it stands today was mostly built in about 1830. As with so many east coast fishing hamlets, the houses present their gable-ends to the sea.

The New Statistical Account (1845) records that: 'There is no regular fishery in the parish, though there is a colony of fishermen at Embo; but they only fish for haddocks, small cods, flounders, etc., which they sell in a fresh state. The women carry the fish in creels on their backs . . . throughout the parish, and sell it as best they can.' At this time there was a fleet of 42 boats fishing from there.

Today Embo is a popular holiday resort and has yachting and water-skiing facilities. There are still a number of fishermen living in the village, but they all fish from other harbours.

The low, sandy coast continues northwards as far as Little Ferry, where a narrow channel connects the sea with Loch Fleet. The loch is crossed by a causeway built by Telford in 1815 and called 'The Mound'. Three miles further on in the small town of **Golspie**, behind which stands an enormous statue of the 1st Duke of Sutherland, a well-known landmark for fishermen, conspicuous for many miles out to sea. Dunrobin Castle, the seat of the dukes, is just to the north of the village. The present building is largely the work of Sir Charles Barry — the architect responsible for the Houses of Parliament. The Dukes had their own railway station at Dunrobin, at which trains would stop on request to unload or collect guests at the castle.

Golspie

The town itself consists of a single street of cottages straggling along the shore, with a number of sidestreets branching inland or down towards the sea. At the southern end of the village is a wooden pier 200 feet long, with a short arm bending southward at its end. In spite of the length of this pier the shore shelves so gradually that there is only four feet of water at high tide. Because of the lack of proper harbour facilities at Golspie, the number and size of boats based there was never very great: even at the height of the herring boom there was only a small fleet.

North of Golspie the coast is cultivated almost down to the beach, and the beach itself is mainly fine white sand — a fact which makes both Golspie and **Brora** very popular holiday resorts. Brora, surrounding the mouth of the river of the same name — one of the finest salmon rivers in Scotland — has been described as the most attractive small industrial town in the country. The older part of the town is built on the south side of the stream and dates mainly from the early 18th century, though it was regarded as a port of note as early as the 16th century, and the small harbour was built parallel to the stream, close to the mouth of the river. It was formerly used for trade as well as for fishing, and it was from here that the first emigrants to New Zealand left the north of Scotland. Since it is

'The people here (i.e. at Embo) are rather above the middle size. They are in general well made and handsome, and the women comely. On the whole they are a moral and religious people; industrious, peaceable and respectful of their superiors . . . . . . poaching and illicit distillation are now scarcely known among them.'

Embo was the site of a battle against the Danes during which Sir Richard de Moravia, the brother of the founder of Dornoch Cathedral, was killed. A large stone near the village commemorates this event.

'Dulse, a brown seaweed rich in iodine, was also eaten. It tasted best roasted or dipped into boiling water. Either way it turned green and this slight cooking made it more digestible.'

The only newspaper published in Sutherland, *The Northern Times*, is based in Golspie. It was founded in 1889 and is issued weekly.

Helmsdale

situated so close to the river's mouth, it is now badly silted up with sand.

The Statistical Account of 1793 records that 'the sea and even the very shore here abounds with excellent fish'. Boats came from near and far, using the harbour and 'never returning home until they have a load of excellent fish'. But by 1839 the New Statistical Account reports that: 'The inhabitants do not take to the sea. They prefer to cultivate their land except during the herring fisheries.'

There were 11 small boats and 23 fishermen working from Brora in 1929, and today there are still a number of small boats based there, fishing mainly for lobsters and crabs. Sea angling trips are also organised from there.

The area at the mouth of the River **Helmsdale** was chosen as a settlement for crofters dispossessed by the Sutherland clearances and was devised as a fishing/farming community, the crofters being divided into those who would work the smallholdings attached to the village and those who would set about the fishing. Few of the families had any knowledge of the sea or tradition of fishing, so fishermen from places like Fraserburgh were encouraged to move there and set an example.

The Duke of Sutherland provided the village with an extensive harbour and very well-equipped curing sheds, superior to any along this coast. Fortunately this development coincided with the beginning of the northern herring boom; boats came to Helmsdale from all over Scotland during the season — upwards of 200 boats packed into the harbour.

Towards the end of the 19th century the fishermen/farmers of Helmsdale found it hard to compete with the better-equipped southern fishermen who used the port, in spite of the fact that they had developed line-fishing for cod and haddock to fill in the gaps between the herring seasons. They could not afford the larger boats and better gear that their competitors used, and when steam drifters began to be adopted in 1900 they found themselves directly unemployed by the curers who owned the boats.

Writing in 1929, Peter Anson remarked that the harbour had 'an almost sinister aspect. The curing stations and coopers' yards standing empty and silent, with closed doors and blocked up windows. . . . The once busy quays where two hundred boats would have been crowding, now grass-grown and ruinous.'

However, in spite of Mr Anson's misgivings, Helmsdale benefited greatly from the arrival of the seine net and the supplanting of the steam drifter by the motor fishing boat. During the 1930s there was a fleet of over a dozen boats registered there; the quays were repaired and the curing sheds restored.

Today the harbour has a resident fleet of boats and two larger boats trawling for white fish. The town's major industry is the processing of crabs, scallops and prawns, and Alex Jappy and Sons Ltd. have an efficient modern plant just north of the harbour which supplies these delicacies, mainly to France. They also have a large tank further up the shore, in which quantities of live lobsters of all sizes are kept until required.

Four miles north of Helmsdale rears the Ord of Caithness, the mountain which forms the border between Sutherland and Caithness. The old road over the Ord, formerly the only path into the northern county, was reckoned to be the most dangerous in Scotland, with seaward precipices so terrifying that 'whenever any of the landed proprietors entered the county, a troop of their tenants assembled on the border and drew the carriage themselves over the hill, a distance of two miles, that nothing might be trusted in such a scene to the discretion of quadrupeds'.

A small pier was built on the north bank of the

In 1850 there were nearly 1,500 men and boys engaged in fishing the district of Lybster between Latheron and Clyth Ness —a coast of only six miles—with a fleet of 313 boats.

A small hut in the churchyard at Latheron was used as a watch house against grave robbers. It was customary for someone to keep watch for 14 days after the funeral to prevent body-snatching.

The road to Thurso branches off the A9 at Latheron. A considerable length of this highway across the moors was laid out in a single day during the 18th century in an exercise planned with military precision by Sir John Sinclair, a local laird. He used every able man and beast, and available stone, in the district.

Dunbeath Water about 1850, lending focus to a scattered village of considerable charm, and providing a facility which might have enabled Dunbeath to rival Lybster or Wick in importance, had the depth of the river been more constant. There are still three full-time lobster boats based there, and a breakwater has recently been constructed to protect the quay against damage by the terrific seas which batter it during the winter.

Surprising as it may seem today, in 1854 there were 89 boats owned by 350 Dunbeath men; eight curers had yards there and there were ice-houses for the preservation of fish.

The village is dominated by the white mass of Dunbeath Castle, a mile to the south and poised spectacularly on the edge of a cliff. The original keep of the castle dates from 1428.

The coast between Latheronwheel and Clyth Ness is formed of steep cliffs backed by grassy braes. The cliffs are between 70 and 170 feet high and rocky ledges stretch out into the sea for some distance. The area is strikingly picturesque, but inhospitable and dangerous: it was only the prodigious quantities of herring to be caught not far from the shore that persuaded so many boats to use the three or four tiny coves along its length as harbours. The name of some of the other coves — like 'The Whaler' and 'The Frenchman' — are grim reminders of ships that foundered there in days gone by.

Neil Gunn, one of Scotland's greatest novelists, was born at Dunbeath in 1891. His early experiences of the sea, fishing and fishermen provided him with much of his material, especially for his best known book, *The Silver Darlings*.

The New Statistical Account has an interesting description of the fishermen's routine during July, August and September when the herring was running: 'The boats usually leave the shore from 5 to 7 o'clock in the afternoon, according to the direction of the wind and the distance at which the fish are supposed to be found, and shoot their nets about dusk.

'In this state they remain, with the boat attached to each drift by means of a head rope, and slowly carried east or west by the tide, until about 3 o'clock the next morning. Then all hands are employed in the hauling of the nets and fish at the boat's stern, till it comes to shore, when they commence the operation of disengaging the fish from the meshes of the net by shaking the nets. . . . The herring being thus separated are immediately landed and deposited in the curing box where a number of women are engaged in gutting and packing them in barrels with salt. Having delivered their fish they bundle up their nets, carry them on shore, and spread them out carefully one over the other. Here they remain to dry, until taken up again in the afternoon to be

Latheronwheel

used as formerly.

'After securing their boats, they return to their homes, take some refreshment and a few hours' repose, as their time permits, and proceed to take up their nets and put to sea again for the next night's fishing. In this manner they proceed for five successive nights every week. Sometimes when the quantity of fish is large, they do not go to bed for days together. . . .'

The harbour at **Latheronwheel** serves the villages of Janetstown and Latheron which stand on the cliffs above. It was built in the 1860s and is one of the most attractive harbours on the entire east coast, a perfect example of how a natural cove can be turned into a safe port by the construction of a sea wall. The burn running through the harbour has caused a certain amount of silting, but there are still five small lobster boats based there.

Christianity is believed to have been brought to Latheron by St Ninian in the 5th century. There is a ruined pre-Reformation chapel there — St Mary's — with doors less than four feet high, and the kirk in the town has had more than its share of idiosyncratic ministers. The Rev. Neil Beaton was suspended by the Presbytery in 1699 when he admitted that he had not administered the sacraments or catechised anyone for 16 years, and that he had danced — or as he put it, 'had gone up and down the room at a wedding'. In 1734 the Rev. James Brodie was suspended for nine months because he 'slit a man's ear for stealing'.

For centuries the **Lybster** district was the most sparsely populated part of Latheron parish. At the close of the 18th century it was inhabited only by a small number of scattered crofters, and no fishing took place until 1793 when a few local men tried fishing for lobsters. So many lobsters were caught that many died in the tightly packed boxes while awaiting the smacks which were to ship them to market.

In 1810 General Patrick Sinclair, the local laird, built a wooden pier within the small creek at the mouth of the Reisgill Burn to allow his tenants to supplement their income by fishing. The project was immediately successful, and in 1833 the

Lybster

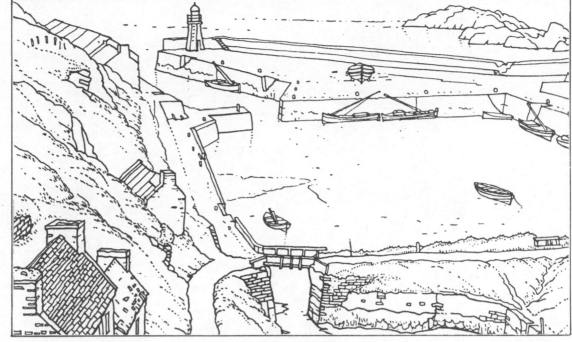

General's successor replaced the jetty with a 300-foot stone pier capable of harbouring large numbers of boats. The situation is very picturesque, with steep grassy braes, dusted with thousands of primroses in spring, forming a bowl to shelter the harbour.

The northern herring boom was in full swing, and by 1840 Lybster had become the third largest station in Scotland, after Wick and Fraserburgh. The first signs of recession appeared in 1882, when the fleet caught almost no fish in the whole season. Steam trawlers appeared in the Moray Firth the same year and the fishermen blamed these for the disappearance of the herring shoals.

In truth, the fish moved north with the Gulf Stream Drift. Herring are cold water creatures and the appearance of pilchards, warm water fish, in the North Sea about this time, indicates a northward movement of the Gulf Stream.

By 1895 only 50 boats were fishing from Lybster, and the arrival of steam drifters in Wick five years later dealt the final death blow to Lybster harbour. The steam drifters travelled great distances to seek out the herring shoals in May and June instead of waiting for them to arrive at the inshore grounds a month later, and the result was that the shoals were broken up and dispersed. Many Lybster men moved to Wick to sign on the steam drifters, others turned to hand-line fishing. The majority resorted to their crofts and endured such hardship that many families emigrated. By 1913 there were only three boats working out of Lybster.

With the arrival of the motorised light fishing trawler the virtues of Lybster's compact and well-protected harbour were again recognised, and the port enjoyed a measure of prosperity. A new quay was opened in 1984, greatly improving the shelter available and providing storage space for tackle, fish boxes and nets, as well as car parking. There are four light trawlers fishing permanently for white fish and about a dozen lobster boats.

Two and a half miles beyond Lybster, Clyth Ness is rounded and just west of the lighthouse is a little ruined pier. **Clyth** harbour sheltered 121 boats in 1855.

The Old Statistical Account says of the place: 'Fishermen on this part of the coast, to get to their boats, descend a huge precipice by winding steps in the face of the rock, by which some lives have been lost, and yet from frequent practice, it is often done without assistance by a blind fisherman in Ulbster.

'To secure their boats from being dashed to pieces against the rocks, particularly in storms and stream tides, the fishermen hang up their yawls by ropes on hooks fixed in the surface of the rock above the level of the water, where they are safely suspended till the weather is fit for going to sea.'

Whaligoe, about two miles further north, is in a similar position. Here the harbour is connected to its village by 365 steps down the cliffside, and the fisherwomen had to carry the catches up this often slippery slope before walking the six miles to market in Wick. The remains of the old curing station can still be seen close to the harbour, and in 1850 there were 35 boats based there.

Much the same story applies to **Scarlet**, two miles further on. The little cove is surrounded by almost perpendicular cliffs, and rocky ledges inside the cove were excavated to form natural quays at which the boats could tie up and unload.

Early this century the harbour was almost destroyed by the sea. At one time there was a

Wick

breakwater extending from the north shore and a pier to the south forming a sheltered basin about half an acre in extent. Sarclet Haven was once regarded as being among the foremost fishing stations on the Caithness coast: even the path down to the harbour is overgrown today and has fallen away in places, and one of the few indications of the port's former prosperity is the scant remains of the curing shed standing by the shore.

The name **Wick** derives from the Norse 'Vik', a bay, and it is likely that the settlement was an important colony for the Vikings: mention of it occurs in a saga of 1140 when 'Earl Rögnvald went over to Caithness and was entertained at Vik by a man named Harold'.

Until the end of the 18th century the town was little more than a cluster of small houses, but with the rise of the east coast fisheries it began to prosper until, in the 1860s, when there were over a thousand boats fishing from there, the place had all the atmosphere of a gold rush town in the American West.

Until 1767 the handful of fishermen who lived at Wick regarded herring merely as bait for white fish, but that year three local merchants fitted out two sloops and fished for herring with great success. The Continent, particularly Eastern Europe, were hungry for the fish and any quantity that could be caught were immediately sold. The man responsible for initiating the rise of Wick as a fishing centre was Sir John Sinclair, M.P. for Caithness from 1780 to 1811. Realising that the sale of herring would go a long way towards improving the lot of the impoverished crofters in his constituency, he brought over a number of Dutch fishermen to teach the locals the secrets of finding, catching and curing the 'silver darlings'. By the end of the century there

were upwards of 200 boats fishing out of Wick during the season, and when the harbour was enlarged by the British Fishery Society in 1808 even more boats made it their base. The model fishing village was built then was named Pulteneytown, after Sir William Pulteney, the director of the British Fishery Society. It was laid out and supervised by Thomas Telford, who named many of the new streets after his friends. The inner harbour was finished in 1810, at a cost of £16,000, and its availability led to such a phenomenal increase in trade that 14 years later it had to be expanded.

The height of Wick's success as a herring town was 1862 when there were 1,122 boats using it as a base, employing 3,800 fishermen and about 4,000 curers, fishwives, coopers, carters, labourers and others associated with the industry. None of the boats were over 30 feet long, though they may have come from ports all over Scotland. They were undecked and offered no protection against wind and waves. The sight of the fleet putting to sea in the late afternoon was memorable:

'About this time (5 p.m.) may be seen hundreds of stalwart fishermen, clad characteristically in north-wester, fearnought jackets and high fishing boots, with kit across the back containing refreshment for the night. In an hour or two the expanse of ocean is studded with a thousand tiny barks, each under canvas and the guidance of the the weather-beaten and experienced skipper, bounding along in the direction of the fishing ground. . . .' (James Thomson, 1849)

'The herring fishing has increased wealth,' wrote the contributor to the New Statistical Account (1845), 'but also wickedness. No care is taken of the 10,000 young strangers of both sexes who are crowded together with the inhabitants within the

On the morning of 19th August 1848 a gale from the south-east struck Wick just as the fleet were heading homewards. Forty-one boats were lost, most of them within a few yards of the harbour.

'A brave little city by the Norse Sea, which may not only be called the 'Wick' but the candle of Northern Scotland . . . the great metropolis of Fishdom.'
(Elin Burritt, an American traveller, 1864)

'As for Wick itself, it is one of the meanest of man's towns, and situate certainly on the baldest of God's bays.'
(Robert Louis Stevenson)

'At all seasons of the year, whisky is drunk in considerable quantities, but during the fishing season enormous potations are indulged in. . . . Snuffing is almost universal among men, and both it and smoking are very common among the women.'

(Rev. Charles Thomson, 1843)

narrow limits of Wick during the six weeks of the fishery, when they are exposed to drink and every other temptation. . . . There is great consumption of spirits, there being 22 public houses in Wick and 23 in Pultneytown . . . Seminaries of Satan and Belial.'

He also recorded that if the fishing was successful, not less than 500 gallons of whisky were consumed in a day.

Robert Louis Stevenson

'Certainly Wick in itself possesses no beauty: bare, grey shores, grim grey houses, grim grey sea; not even the greenness of a tree. . . .

'In Wick I have never heard anyone greet his neighbour with the usual "Fine day" or "Good morning". Both come shaking their heads, and both say, "Breezy, breezy!". And such is the atrocious climate that the remark is almost invariably justified by the fact.

'The streets are full of highland fishers, lubberly, stupid, inconceivably lazy and heavy to move. You bruise against them, tumble over them, elbow them against the wall — and all to no purpose; they will not budge; and you are forced to leave the pavement every step.'

from a letter to his mother, September 1868

During the winter of 1871 the breakwater was broken up by the sea, with damage estimated at £140,000. So prosperous was the town that the money to repair it and to further enlarge the harbour was quickly found. Robert Louis Stevenson's father was responsible for building the new basin.

Eventually the herring disappeared from the waters close to Wick, as they did from all other parts of the coast. The harbour was quick to adopt steam drifters to pursue the fish into northern waters, but by 1911 the fishing fleet had halved in size. In 1928 there was still a sizeable fleet of 22 steam drifters, 19 large motor drifters and 14 other vessels, and there are 200 boats registered at Wick today, although the vast majority of these are small lobster boats fishing out of ports and creeks up and down the coast: there are only 12 seine netters and nine light trawlers fishing from Wick harbour itself.

Boat Registration

Fishermen today are as superstitious as ever about the number allocated to their boat by the Fisheries Officer in their home port. Sometimes owners hold on to a particular number once they have sold their boat, a practice which is not encouraged by the registrar. If a boat moves to a different port of registration it is usual for her to be re-registered there. Some numbers — 13 for example (although WK13 was specifically requested by one fisherman) — remain unused in the register due to the refusal of the owners to take them.

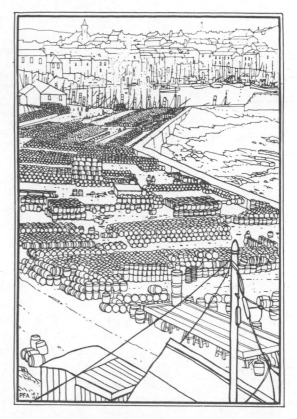

The town has many buildings which recall the last century and the importance of the port, as well as three boatbuilders, a large fish merchant, a fish market and an interesting Heritage Centre which specialises in objects and information relating to fishing.

The Boy Andrew, a Wick boat, has consistently landed more fish than any other boat in Scotland since 1977. There have been three boats of the same name all owned by Norman Bremner and fishing out of Peterhead. The present vessel — at 85 feet the largest in Wick's fleet — was the 'Top Scots Boat' in 1982 and 1983, which implies that she has landed more fish than any other boat of comparable size in Europe. Her skipper, Andrew Bremner, is the owner's son: he was 26 in 1983.

Just north of Wick there were formerly a number of hamlets associated with tiny creeks, or 'goes', all of which harboured handfuls of fishing boats. Greengoe, Ullergoe, Papigoe and Elzie are only marked on detailed maps today, though Broadhaven and **Staxigoe** are still used by local lobster boats.

There was a time when letters to Wick had to be addressed 'Wick by Staxigoe', such was the village's importance in relation to its neighbour. It was one of the earliest Caithness ports: grain was exported from here in the 17th century, and in 1651 one of Oliver Cromwell's frigates captured a Dutch ship leaving the harbour with a cargo of fish, tallow, hides and beef, and letters to Royalist exiles in Holland.

The rocky coast of low cliffs continues as far as Noss Head, surmounted by a lighthouse and a very striking outline from the sea. Beyond the Head is Sinclair Bay, and just behind the

e Harbour Master's fice on the pierhead Wick is a rare gem Edwardiana. Un-ered since it was first lt in the 1900s, even wn to the wallpaper d paintwork, it has a ique atmosphere as ll as still performing important duties.

The Fourth Earl of Caithness imprisoned his son in Girnigoe Castle suspecting him of having plotted his death. The unfortunate boy died of 'famine and vermine'.

On a July evening in 1944 three men sailed from Keiss and anchored their drift-nets in Sinclair Bay. The following morning they hauled in nearly seven cran of herring: this was the last catch of herring ever landed at Keiss.

John Nicholson was related to the Groats, of John O'Groats, and many of his descendants still live in Auckengill. His work as an archaeologist and a sculptor was famous, and there are many examples of it in and around the village.

'Rainy, rainy
Rattlestanes
Dinna rain on me
Rain on John O'Groats
hoose
Far across the sea!'

(Traditional)

lighthouse are the spectacular ruins of Girnigoe and Sinclair Castles, the latter of which was the residence of the Earls of Caithness.

The stretch of coast between Wick and John O'Groats is among the earliest inhabited parts of Scotland. Excavations have indicated that the Middle Stone Age inhabitants of the area continued in their primitive way of life long after more advanced cultures — New Stone Age and Iron Age — were flourishing in other parts of the country.

Although Wick was far and away the most important port on the Caithness coast, several of the smaller villages also enjoyed a boom at the same time. In 1855, for example, **Keiss** harbour was the home port for 49 vessels, manned by 180 men and backed up by seven coopers, 96 gutters and packers, 21 fish curers and 190 netmakers. As bigger boats took over and the smaller harbours were squeezed out of business, the fishermen turned to white fish and to lobsters and crabs to earn their living. The men of Keiss were remarkably successful in catching crabs: in 1928 only five harbours on the entire East Coast landed more crabs than they did, and the nearest one was Crail in Fife.

The harbour has an inner and an outer basin — still used by lobster and salmon fishermen — and the remains of the curing yards and ice-house stand witness to the industry which was there previously.

Less important but no less picturesque is the little harbour below the village of **Auckengill**. The beach is covered in pebbles and unusual flat rocks, and the concrete pier, shaped like a lightning flash, combines with the landscape to remind one of a painting by Paul Nash or Graham Sutherland.

Just above the pier is a small dry-stone hut, still piled with maritime detritus; on the brae behind are two curious monuments, one was a beacon to guide boats into the harbour; the other, surmounted by a stone lion, formerly housed a barometer. They were the work of John Nicholson, painter, sculptor and archaeologist, who lived in the village and died in 1934.

Beyond Nybster Head, two miles north of Auckengill, the Bay of Freswick opens up, on the north side of which is the little harbour of **Skirza**, also called Freswick Harbour.

The harbour is created by a recently repaired stone pier which runs out at right angles to the shore for about 50 yards and shelters a small, stony beach. Behind it is a dilapidated curing shed used as a store for fishing gear and the harbour provides a base for a couple of old yoles — half-decked boats about 20 feet long, built in a style which had been developed in Orkney while the East Coast of Scotland were using Fifies, Scaffies and Zulus. **John O'Groats** has had a ferry link with the Orkney Islands since the 16th century and the harbour there was of considerable importance to local crofting fishermen, although it was never very populous. It has recently been expanded and improved and now provides a haven for three full-time trawlers and five lobster yoles.

John O'Groat's House, to give the place its full name, was an octagonal building on the shore of the Pentland Firth. It is said that in about 1500 a Dutchman named Jan de Groot settled in this part of the world. The family prospered and multiplied until there were eight distinct branches all living in the district, known for their loyalty towards one another and their

John O'Groats

'he contrary tides and
urrent form here a
nost tremendous
ontest; yet by the
kilfullness of the
eople are passed with
reat safety in the
arrow little boats I
ow lying on the shore.'
Thomas Pennant, 1769)

urope's only cowrie is
ast up on the beach at
ohn O'Groats along
ith many other shells.
he cowries are known
s 'John O'Groats
uckies', and are used
y local jewellers and
ilversmiths.

friendliness to strangers. Then one day, when the whole family were having a party, a violent quarrel broke out concerning who had the right to sit at the head of the table, close to the door. Bloodshed was only averted by the father, Jan, saying that he would settle the point of issue to the satisfaction of them all before their next gathering.

He then built an octagonal house, with a door and a window on each side and containing an octagonal table. Thus each family could enter by their own door and take their seat at the table. John O'Groat's House no longer stands today, although its site can still be seen and the neighbouring hotel, built in 1875, has an appropriate octagonal tower. The parallels

between the story and the legend of the Round Table are apparent, and some hold that Jan was a ferryman who charged extortionate amounts to carry his passengers over to Orkney until he was ordered by magistrates to fix the fare at four pence (about 1½ new pence), which gave the name to the little silver coin, the groat.

Although John O'Groats is not the northernmost point of the British mainland (this distinction belongs to Dunnet Head, some 10 miles to the west), it is generally recognised to be Land's End's opposite number. Even the facility of modern travel cannot altogether banish the feeling of achievement when one has come this far.

Keiss

THE ORKNEY ISLANDS

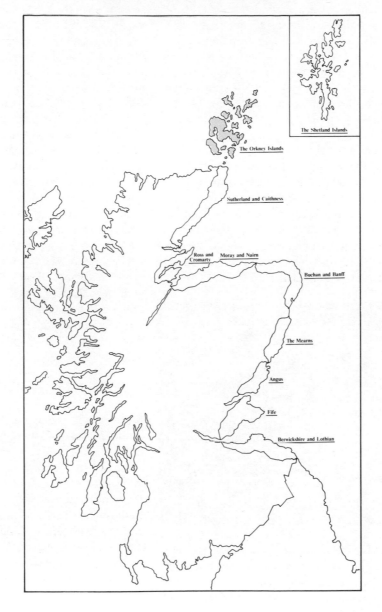

The Shetland Islands

The Orkney Islands

Sutherland and Caithness

Ross and Cromarty   Moray and Nairn

Buchan and Banff

The Mearns

Angus

Fife

Berwickshire and Lothian

ORKNEY is a group of 67 islands covering an area of 376 square miles. Apart from the island of Hoy, which rises, heather clad, to 1,570 feet, they are low and gently undulating; the rich soil makes for good farmland and everywhere green fields stretch to the very edge of precipitous cliffs or sandy beaches.

It is difficult to imagine the terrain of Orkney 5,000 years ago, but it is supposed that, with the addition of more trees (today there is only a handful of woods, mostly situated around the larger houses), it was as fertile then as now. Certainly the islands are a 'veritable museum of antiquities' — it is said that there are three sites of historical interest to every square mile!

The earliest example of a 'fishing village' in Scotland is the wonderfully preserved prehistoric habitation of **Skara Brae**. Occupied from between 3100 B.C. and 2500 B.C., the village was ultimately buried — and thus preserved — by blown sand. Six houses remain perfectly intact, complete with stone furnishings, and kitchen refuse found on the site shows that fish and shellfish formed an important part of the villagers' diet.

The prevailing historical ambience of the islands is Norse. By the eighth century Orkney had been colonised by Vikings and farmers from Scandinavia, and the islands only came under the rule of Scotland in 1468, when they were pledged to the Scots Crown in a marriage settlement. Numerous remains from the 11th and 12th century — the golden age of Norse culture — remind of this long occupation, and contemporary place names, language, customs and traditions all owe much to Scandinavia.

Although physically sundered from cultural and social developments on the mainland of Scotland, Orkney kept up to date on account of the importance of its port at Kirkwall. Until the American War of Independence, the British Government required all ships sailing to or from colonial harbours to call at a British Customs port and pay a levy. Kirkwall was one such port. Moreover, since the Hudson Bay Company had opened up the northern route to America, through the Pentland Firth, all ships bound for Northern Europe — Amsterdam, St Petersburg, Bergen, Hamburg and so on — were obliged to call at Kirkwall to pay their dues. Later Stromness was also made a Customs port.

During the 19th century a fishing industry developed in the islands. In 1837, 710 herring boats worked from Stronsay and Stromness yet fishing as a livelihood was not highly thought of and most of these boats were generally operated by outsiders. By the late 19th century the industry had grown, and in July and August up to 5,000 fishermen, gutters and packers came to the islands. Still, fishing was not an activity which was generally pursued by the Orcadians: in contrast to the Shetlanders who regarded themselves as fishermen with smallholdings they tended to be farmers who occasionally fished.

Today, however, the industry is again growing, mostly based on shellfish. Until quite recently, crabs — known locally as 'partans' — were tossed back into the sea but plants in Westray, Rousay, Kirkwall and Stromness now process, freeze and export crabmeat. White fishing is also flourishing, with new boats up to 120 feet in length catching skate, cod and haddock.

For convenience this chapter had been divided into three sections: The Mainland, The South Isles and The North Isles.

THE MAINLAND

Kirkwall was one of the earliest established Norse trading towns, and 'Kirkjuvagr' is first recorded in the *Orkneyinga Saga* of the mid-11th century. The name means 'Church Bay of the Vikings' and indicates the presence of a Celtic church here when the Norsemen arrived.

In those days Kirkwall was the only community of any size in all Orkney, and it remained so until the growth of Stromness in the 17th century — indeed, although Stromness at one time had a great population, Kirkwall has always remained the centre of power and its handsome buildings reflect this influence.

Kirkwall

The title 'Jarl' is not synonymous with the English and Scots 'Earl'. The rulers of Orkney were petty kings, often related by blood to the kings of Norway and, at a later period, by marriage to the Royal House of Scotland.

The meaning of the name 'Orkney' has never been established with certainty — the first syllable probably derives from 'orkn', the Old Icelandic for 'seal'. 'Ey' is Old Norse and means 'islands'. 'Islands of the Seal' is therefore a plausible explanation.

'Kirkwall stands along an Arm of the Sea . . . and consists of one Street three Quarters of a Mile long, in which there are about 300 Families. All the Houses are built of Stone; some of them tolerably handsome both within and without, and, for the most Part, have a small Kitchen-garden behind. A Brook crosses the Street towards the north End, over which there is a Bridge of one Arch, with a parapet wall on either side. . . .'

(Murdoch Mackenzie, 1750)

The town grew up behind a harbour which stood on a narrow neck of water known as the Peerie Sea. Before 1858 this little basin was separated from Kirkwall Bay, into which it gave, by a peninsula of shingle beach called an 'ayre'. Traffic entered through a gap called an 'oyce'. Today the basin is entirely landlocked and there are no signs of the original harbour, the wharfs and quays having been largely replaced by a small power station.

The houses of the old port of Kirkwall presented their gable-ends to the Peerie Sea, in the manner of so many east coast villages, and long narrow properties ran up from the shore towards the cathedral. Although the original harbour has been cleared, enough old houses and narrow, twisting streets survive for the town to be ranked among the best preserved medieval burghs in Scotland.

It is dominated by the red sandstone mass of St Magnus' Cathedral, founded in 1137 by the Jarl Rognvald in memory of his martyred uncle — the Jarl Magnus. The bones of both are entombed in its columns. Surprisingly, the cathedral is not owned by any particular denomination, having been granted to the citizens of Kirkwall by royal charter in 1486.

Nearby are the remains of the Bishop's Palace where King Hakon of Norway died in 1263, after his ill-fated invasion of Scotland, and the palace of Earl Patrick Stewart, one of the finest examples of Renaissance architecture in the country.

In spite of its beauty, the town has had its detractors. When Sir Walter Scott visited in 1814, as part of his tour with the Northern Lighthouse Commissioners, he wrote:

> We have now got to Kirkwall, and needs
> I must stare,
> When I think that in verse I have once
> call'd it fair;
> 'Tis a base little borough, both dirty and
> mean,
> There is nothing to hear, and there's
> nought to be seen,
> Save a church, where of old times, a
> prelate harangued
> And a palace that's built by an earl that
> was hanged."

By contrast, Robert Louis Stevenson later wrote: "I know of nothing so suggestive of legend, so full of superstition, so stimulating to a weird imagination as the rocks and corners and by-ways of such a church as St Magnus in Kirkwall."

The present harbour at Kirkwall was mainly built during the 1850s, although some parts of its are considerably older. The Corn Slip, for example — a small pier near the main harbour — was devoted to the export of grain. During the 18th and early 19th centuries huge quantities of oatmeal and bere travelled from here to the West Highlands, Ireland, Norway and the Netherlands, and even as far afield as Spain and Portugal. Facing the harbour stands a 17th century granary in which the Yarls garnered their taxes, called 'Skatts' and paid in grain.

Today the port is a base for a fleet of about twenty lobster boats and three trawlers. A recently established local factory processes white fish and shellfish, and there is a curing firm which smokes salmon. Passenger ferries leave from here for Shetland and the North Isles and cargo boats land coal, cement, oil and grain and load up with farm produce and cattle.

The Ba' Game

Each Christmas and New Year's Day an obscure form of football is played between the men of the harbour and surrounding area (the Doonies) and those of the Laverock and Victoria Street end (the Uppies). The game often involves as many as 150 men who struggle in a loose scrum to force a ball either into the harbour or to a goal at the old castle. The struggle continues for as long as it takes to score the 'goal' — sometimes all day. The game is of great antiquity, first being referred to in the Norse Saga of Gisli the Outlaw.

North-west of Kirkwall, the wide Bay of Firth was once well stocked with oysters. At its head is **Finstown**, and the well-built stone pier there was once used by both oyster boats and cargo vessels. Such was the demand for shellfish, however, that the bay was over-fished and the breeding grounds destroyed. There is no fishing from Finstown today.

Orkney Tee Names

Each district in the islands had its own nickname. Tradition holds that many of these date from the building of the Cathedral and were given according to the provisions brought with the several detachments:
Kirkwall—Starlings
Stromness—Bloody Puddings
Birsay—Dogs or Hoes (small sharks)
Hoy—Hawks
Rousay—Mares
Wyre—Whelks
Westray—Auks
Stronsay—Limpets

The stone pier at **Tingwall**, some six miles further north, is the ferry point for the island of Rousay and provides a base for at least one lobster boat. The north-western shoulder of the Mainland is Brough Head, a mile east of which is a small bay set with jagged sandstone slabs. At the head of the bay is a tiny pebble beach, formerly the 'noust' or boat-beach of **Skippie Geo**. 'Geo' means an inlet, but all that remains today of the sailhouses that used to stand above the beach is a stretch of fragile

---

'Peerie' is a Shetland word meaning 'small'. The correct Orkney version is 'peedie'.

The small hilly island of Guirsay, which lies about a mile off the coast between Finstown and Tingwall, was the home of one of Orkney's most notorious Vikings — Sweyn Asleifson. The remains of Sweyn's drinking hall at Langskaill can still be seen. (See Rousay.)

There was a very common proverb in the Orkneys: 'Giff Bessie say it is weill it is weill'. The bessie referred to was one Bessie Skebister, who claimed that she knew whether any fishing boats were in danger or not. . . . She was strangled and burned for various improbable offences, one of which was that of riding on the back of one James Sandieson, and flying with him through the air to Norway and Zetland, with a bridle in his mouth.

Stromness

dry-stone wall.

The Point of Buckquoy is about half a mile from Skippie Geo and affords a fine view over the Brough of Birsay. Behind it is the hamlet of **Birsay** itself, dominated by the ruins of the late 16th century Earl's Palace, built for Mary Queen of Scots' half-brother, the bastard Earl Robert Stewart. The fields around here are very fertile, and the adjacent sea was so abundant with fish that the crofters of Birsay were known as 'dogs' from the number of dogfish they caught.

At the north-west tip of the mainland, and connected by tidal causeway, lies the tilted green island known as Brough of Birsay. This was formerly the seat of Orcadian administration and the remains of the mighty Jarl Thorfinn's hall, dating from the 11th century, are still apparent along with the nucleus of the old Norse town, a cathedral church and a bishop's palace.

Mar Wick ('Wick' comes from 'Vik', a bay) is a gentle sandy bay, sheltered to the north by the bulk of Marwick Head. But for the fact that it is entirely blocked at low tide by outlying reefs, it would have made a fine boat beach: as it is the fisher-farmers of the district had to use the tiny creek of **Sand Geo**, half a mile further south.

Sand Geo is an improbable harbour. Its narrow entrance is encompassed by rough sandstone slabs, set diagonally into the sea bed and constantly washed by Atlantic surf. The tiny noust is reached only by a steep descent, yet above it are three recently — and very well — restored fishermen's huts. Dry-stone built and roofed with turf, these low boat sheds once more accommodate the creels and tackle of local fishermen.

The coast continues rocky for another mile and a half until it opens out into the beautiful Bay of Skaill — a lovely arc of white sand and dunes and the site of the Stone Age settlement of **Skara Brae**, already referred to. Close by the prehistoric village stands the impressive mansion house of Skaill, erected in the early 17th century and one of the oldest occupied houses in Orkney. The house is reputed to be haunted by the ghost of a small boy whose sole ambition was to build an island of his own. For years he rowed back and forth across the Loch of Skaill carrying loads of stones which he dumped in the middle. Eventually a small hump of dry land appeared. The boy sat on this island and promptly died. The tiny island is still visible in the middle of the loch.

If Sand Geo is an improbable harbour, **Yesnaby** is impossible. Sheer, crumbling cliffs, battered by the full force of the Atlantic are suddenly riven by a tiny creek, at the head of which is a stony beach. It seems incredible that fishermen braved the surf and outlying skerries to enter this little haven, for the smallest misjudgement in bad weather would dash them against the cliffs. Yet fish from here they did, and remnants of tackle sheds stand witness to their courage.

The inlet of Hamnavoe, at the head of which

stands **Stromness**, was much esteemed by the Vikings as a natural harbour. By 1603 French and Spanish ships travelling to the New World were using it for shelter, and the first houses built at Stromness were erected about this time by the sons of the local landowners to provision and do business with these visitors.

The town grew slowly. In 1670 there were still only 13 houses, but during the following century it prospered and expanded, and its wealthy sons bought estates all over Orkney.

The reason for the prosperity was trade. Throughout much of the 18th century the south coast of England was infested by French privateers, and the northern route to America, through the Pentland Firth, became more and more popular. Between 1757 and 1760, for example, Stromness received £14,000 in duty from ships arriving from America, and by the time the southern route again became safe for shipping at the end of the Seven Years War in 1763, the port's reputation was secure.

Houses were built along the shore, presenting their backs to the sea, each with its own small pier and slipway, and behind this the town grew up in a ribbon of closely packed narrow houses. Many of these houses still stand today and most of those that have been built since have been designed in keeping with their 18th century neighbours, making Stromness an unusually attractive town.

Near the south end of the main street there is an interesting plaque beside an old well — 'Site of Login's Well. There watered here the Hudson Bay Coy's ships 1670-1891; Capt. Cook's vessels *Resolution* and *Discovery*, 1780; Sir John Franklin's ships *Erebus* and *Terror* on Arctic Exploration, 1845; also the merchant vessels of Former Days. Well sealed up, 1931.'

Sir John Franklin's ships were on their voyage to the Arctic from which they were never to return. Captain Cook's vessels were on their homeland voyage from the Pacific.

Prosperity increased through the activities of the Hudson's Bay Company. By the beginning of the 19th century the company's vessels had adopted the practice of remaining in Stromness for a fortnight in June every year to prepare for the voyage to Canada. Three vessels of up to 400 tons sailed annually with cargoes of clothing, guns, powder and axes which were bartered for furs. Furthermore, the company employed many

The word 'quoy' appears all over Orkney. It refers to a farm, or, more correctly, the virgin land before it was farmed.

Hamnavoe means 'The haven within the bay' in Norse.

On Marwick Head stands the memorial to Field Marshall Lord Kitchener who perished near this spot during the First World War when his ship, **H.M.S. Hampshire**, struck a mine.

The Loch of Skaill is the only private loch in mainland Orkney. Since there are so many other lochs available to fishermen in the islands —all free—Orkney is a haven for freshwater fishermen. International fly fishing tournaments are held there, and the islands' wild brown trout are reputed to be the best in Britain. Sea trout is fished in salt water in the early spring and late autumn.

Stromness

There are staggering views from the clifftops of Yesnaby, and the highest of them is marked by a 'castle'.

Some people swear that they have seen America from here, but it is more likely to have been the mystical island of 'Heather-Blether' which, according to legend, floats these northern waters, warning any who catch sight of it of their own impending doom.

Orcadians — principally because they were willing to work longer for less money than other recruits. Most came from the Stromness area and were respected for their sobriety: at one stage, no fewer than 75 per cent of the Hudson's Bay Company's employees were from Orkney.

The royal charter of 1670 required the Hudson's Bay company to explore and prospect the vast territories of northern Canada and one of the most distinguished pioneers was Dr John Rae, of Hall of Clestran in Orphir, who made five epic journeys into the Arctic between 1846 and 1854. During these travels he added over 1,000 miles of previously uncharted coastline to his maps. His remains lie within an extravagant and very unusual tomb in St Magnus Cathedral, surmounted by a larger than life-size effigy of the explorer sprawling with his gun and gear.

Around 1760 Stromness had also become a supply base for whaling ships bound for the Davis Straits and the North Atlantic. The town was thus able to benefit from the great whaling bonanza between 1790 and 1830. Until the beginning of the 20th century whaling was a common occupation for Stromness men, and by the time the northern seas had been emptied of whales, herring fishing and its associated trades had taken over as the principal occupation.

In the last decades of the 19th century the town expanded considerably. A new pier was built. Curing yards appeared to the south of the town. Coopers, chandlers, sailmakers and packers proliferated. However, the industry was wildly unpredictable; boom times were followed by years of ruin, and by 1914 Stromness had declined into a minor fishing port with very little commercial traffic.

The situation today is much improved. The town boasts two large purse-seiners, both over 120 ft. long, a pair of 70 ft. trawlers and a couple of 40 ft. lobster boats. As well as this there are about a dozen smaller boats based there which are worked by part-timers. In the summer this fleet is swelled by pleasure boats of all kinds and also by vessels used by divers exploring the wrecks in Scapa Flow. There is, regretfully, no fish market at Stromness, although there is a fish processing plant and a lobster pond.

John Gow, the Pirate

In the early part of the 18th century the infamous John Gow lived in Stromness. His father, a merchant, had come from Caithness and built a house on the east side of the harbour. Young Gow went to sea and little was heard of him for several years.

Then, in January 1725, a substantial merchant vessel under his command anchored in Stromness. Feasting and drinking, ashore and aboard, followed. Some time later, the truth leaked out that Gow and his crew had mutinied a year before and murdered their officers. They were now pirates. (In fact, of the four ships they had boarded since they had become pirates, two had cargoes of timber and one a hold full of fish!)

The crew soon realised that the townsfolk knew the

97

truth, and, after plundering the House of Clestrain, they weighed anchor and quickly departed. Their ship foundered on the Calf of Eday, however; they were captured and taken to London. After the trial, Gow and nine of his crew were executed.

Gow's story interested Daniel Defoe, who wrote *The Pirate* after hearing it from an old woman in Stromness.

THE SOUTH ISLES

Scapa Flow was one of the principal achorages in the U.K. during both world wars. It was here that convoys collected and their naval escorts sheltered prior to journeying to Russia or across the North Atlantic. It was here that the seventy ships of the German High Seas Fleet were taken at the end of the Great War, only to be scuttled by their own crews in 1919. And it was here that the battleship *Royal Oak* was sunk by a German submarine in 1939.

Indeed the whole vast bay is a cemetery for warships, some of which, like *Royal Oak* (marked by a perch a mile off Scapa Pier), are official sea graves. In recent years, diving on other wrecks in the bay has become very popular, and all except seven of the High Seas Fleet have been salvaged for scrap metal.

Burray Island

The village of **St Mary's** is situated on the southern shore of the east mainland. Two parallel rows of attractive cottages are separated from the Bay of Ayre by a road and look out over a fine stone pier. A number of pleasure boats are based there during the summer, but no commercial fishing takes place from the harbour.

It was remarked in the New Statistical Account that when the men of St Mary's put to sea they always turned their boats in the direction of the sun's course: 'to move in the opposite way would be considered improper, if not dangerous'. This superstition has been noted in several other ports on the east coast.

To the east of the village is the northernmost Churchill Barrier — the first of the great causeways built during World War II to close off the eastern entry to Scapa Flow. The Barriers were built by a team of Irish navvies, assisted by 550 Italian prisoners-of-war who were brought to Orkney after being captured in North Africa. The P.o.W.s lived in a camp on the tiny island of LAMB HOLM, between the first and second Barriers, and in 1943 they converted a nissen hut there into a Roman Catholic chapel using scrap materials and such ingenuity that the place is now one of Orkney's principal visitor attractions.

The man responsible for the decoration of the Italian Chapel was Domenico Chiocchetti, a private soldier esteemed for his calm and spirituality, and gifted to an unusual degree as a craftsman. The inside of the hut was lined with hardboard and then painted with illusionistic titles, beams and frescoes.

The Barriers connect the Mainland with BURRAY, an attractive island which was formerly an active fishing centre. The western part of the island is hilly, and the eastern part well cultivated. A magnificent stretch of sandy beach — known as 'The Bu' — arcs along the shore on the latter coast, close to the old family seat of the Stewarts of Burray, originally built by the notorious Patrick Stewart in the 17th century. There are still net warehouses at the pierhead of **Burray Village**, and the old herring station buildings here are now a bar and restaurant. The adjacent boatyard, which has been run by the same family for five generations, is one of the principal boatbuilders in Orkney and still builds first-rate fishing boats.

The minister of South Ronaldsay and Burray noted in the Old Statistical Account that twice in the past few years he had been interrupted when on the point of baptising a small girl before a boy. The parishioners feared that if the girl was baptised first she would grow up with a strong beard and the boy would have none. Also, marriage dates were fixed only after a study of the moon and tides.

Some say that SOUTH RONALDSAY is the most beautiful of the Orkney islands — certainly it is visited by more people than any other.

On the gently undulating hills and valleys the excellent land has been cultivated for centuries. *The Orkneyinga Saga* refers to the island often and King Hakon's fleet were lying at anchor in St Margaret's Bay, prior to the invasion of Scotland in 1263, when an eclipse of the sun took place.

Perfectly situated at the head of this bay is **St Margaret's Hope**, arguably the most picturesque village of all those covered by this book. Like

St Margaret's Hope

Stromness, the main street is separated from the sea by a row of houses, and behind this the little village piles up the hillside in higgledy piggledy rows of pink and grey sandstone houses. Most of the buildings are tall and narrow — a feature of Orcadian architecture — and have traditional crow-step gables: most were built in the 17th and 18th centuries.

> The ill-fated Maid of Norway died at St Margaret's Hope — it is said from seasickness — in November 1290. She was only seven years old and was travelling to marry Prince Edward of England (later Edward II). Her mother had been the daughter of Alexander III (1249-86), and on his death she was proclaimed Queen of Scots: her premature end precipitated the Wars of Independence.

St Margaret's Hope provides sheltered moorings for a number of small craft and many of the locals fish for lobsters. Somewhat surprisingly, the pier in the village is so small as to be scarcely usable, however, on the west side of the bay a substantial stone pier was erected in the 18th century by Selby & Co. of London, who, with the Northumbrian Fishing Society, used the place as a base from which to fish lobsters. This pier is now used by an oil company for servicing vessels working on the oil terminal at Flotta. There is one full-time fishing boat based there.

> 'Petty theft is very frequent. There are no Justices of Peace to punish this vice; and if there were, it would be extremely difficult to convict the delinquent; because there is a very general belief, that whosoever is concerned in bringing the guilty to punishment, will never thrive.'
> **(Old Statistical Account, South Ronaldsay and Burray)**

Widewall Bay, a mile south-west of St Margaret's Hope, was also used by the English companies, and the village of **Herston** on the west side of the bay was built specifically for the curing of herring.

Herston is no more than a handful of attractive stone cottages straggling along a pebble beach. The tiny slipway tells little about the frenzy of

activity that went on here during the herring boom, though it is still used today by a number of lobster boats, and creels are piled up outside every cottage. On the beach is the rotting hull of a sizeable fishing boat.

Burwick, the southernmost hamlet on South Ronaldsay, is really no more than a cluster of semi-derelict farm buildings, however, there is plenty of evidence for the pebble beach having been used — and continuing to be used — as a fishing station. Half a dozen old winches are set into the turf above the steeply shelving beach, and beside them are four or five moldering hulls. Nearby is a substantial stone boathouse and slipway, used to lodge the boat which services the Pentland Skerries lighthouse.

A lengthy girder pier was built on the east side of Bur Wick in 1982 to accommodate the small ferry which runs to John O'Groats during the summer months.

> At Burwick there is a fine, low, 17th century church, built almost on the beach itself and crowded about with grave-stones — many of which mark the graves of crofting fishermen.
> The church has no windows on the landward side: this was the side that the black north wind blew from, bringing evil and bad luck.

Due west of St Margaret's Hope is the island of FLOTTA, the centre of the modern oil industry which has brought such prosperity to Orkney, and beyond Flotta, the mass of the island of HOY.

Hoy is heather-covered and hilly, unlike the rest of Orkney. Its distinctive outline dominates Scapa Flow and supplies the view from the southern mainland, rising to 1,500 feet. On the Atlantic side of the island are the highest perpendicular cliffs in Britain, plunging into the sea for 1,140 feet at St John's Head, and nearby stands the famous landmark of the Old Man of Hoy.

The Old Man of Hoy is a red sandstone column of rock, rising out of the sea for 450 feet two miles south of St John's Head. Until the middle of the last century, there was a second 'leg' connecting it to the sea bed, thus making the stack even more 'man-like'.

The walking in the hills behind St John's Head is famous, particularly around the beautiful hamlet of **Rackwick**, acknowledged to be among the most scenic places in Orkney. This was formerly a thriving crofting community and the people were famous for their salted cod. Some of the cottages have been restored, but many others stand roofless and ruined.

On the southern end of Hoy, **Longhope** was an anchorage favoured by the ships of many nations, waiting for suitable weather to carry them through the treacherous Pentland Firth. On each side of the entrance to the bay stand Martello Towers, built during the Napoleonic Wars to protect ships trading into the Baltic against the depradations of American privateers. The ships would wait for convoy escorts at Longhope.

A mile or so north of Longhope is the famous base of **Lyness** — the naval nerve-centre for Scapa Flow during the last war, but today a bleak and depressing sight with debris from the base lying decayed and forgotten along the shore.

It has long been hoped to develop Lyness and to make use of some of the wartime detritus to create a museum and 'Interpretation Centre' devoted to the naval anchorage at Scapa Flow. At the time of writing this plan is again being considered.

On the night of 17th March 1969, the Longhope lifeboat, *T.G.B.*, was lost with the eight members of her volunteer crew. The *T.G.B.* (the name commemorated the anonymous donor's initials) was called out to assist the S.S. *Irene*, a Liberian ship, struggling off South Ronaldsay.

In a ferocious sea with visibility reduced almost to nil and a Force 9 gale blowing. *T.G.B.* capsized near the Pentland Skerries. S.S. *Irene* grounded and her crew was rescued. The following afternoon the lifeboat was found quite close to her base. She has since been refitted and now serves in the Arran Islands.

THE NORTH ISLES

The North Isles of Orkney fall naturally into two groups — the Inner Isles and the Outer Isles. Unlike the South Isles they are not connected to the mainland, but there are regular ferry services from Kirkwall and Tingwall, and between the islands themselves.

Birsay Cod

1 cod

Stuffing:
1 tbsp chopped suet
2 tbsps breadcrumbs
chopped parsley
1 beaten egg
juice of 1 lemon and some grated rind seasoning

Coat with melted butter and brown breadcrumbs.

Wash fish thoroughly and mix all the ingredients for stuffing. Bind the stuffing with the egg and press into the fish, tying the fish at the tail and head. Brush with melted butter and sprinkle with breadcrumbs. Place fish in a baking tray with some melted butter and cook for half an hour at 350°, basting frequently. Garnish with parsley before serving.

Farming dominates the coastal lands of the island of ROUSAY; the interior is hilly and inhospitable, and some of Orkney's finest trout can be caught in the hill lochs and burns.

Near the shore on the western side of the island are the remains of the homestead of Brough, seat of the Craigies (c. 1500), and along the shore to the east is the long-deserted parish church of St Mary. It was from here that Jarl Paul Hakonsen was kidnapped by Sweyn Asleifson and never seen again (see Gairsay).

Rousay is particularly dense in archaeological remains, with many brochs and cairns being located on the island. Indeed, the 'stalled cairns' of the second millenium B.C. here reach their most perfect development.

Lying east of Rousay is the smaller, flatter island of EGILSAY. Very conspicuous on the top of the island is the unusual 12th century round tower of the church of St Magnus — the only surviving example of its kind in Orkney and an indication of Irish influence.

Legend has it that the Jarl Magnus, after whom the cathedral in Kirkwall is named, spent the night of 15th April 1117 praying in the church. He had arranged to meet his co-ruler and first cousin, the Jarl Hakon, in Egilsay next morning.

When Hakon arrived with a large band of warriors it was clear that any discussion was to be done at sword-point. The gentle Magnus offered to leave the islands forever and go on a pilgrimage to the Holy Land. When this was unacceptable, he offered to have himself imprisoned in Scotland, or even maimed and put in a 'dark dungeon' in Orkney.

Nothing would satisfy Hakon's supporters but Magnus' death, but no one would execute the deed. In the end, Hakon ordered his cook to do it. Magnus blessed the man and then told him to 'hew on my head a great wound, for it is not seemly to behead chiefs like thieves'.

On old charts, the island of WYRE is called 'Viera' — a Latinised version of the ancient name 'Vigr' (spearhead). Two 12th century ruins are of special interest — the chapel, and Cubbie Roo's castle — a mound, on which was built the fortress of the mighty warrior Kolbein Hrugga. Its name is a degraded form of the Viking's own.

Scallops, crabs and lobsters are caught by the fishermen of these islands and processed at a co-operatively owned fish factory at Rousay Pier. Visitors are welcome and fresh or frozen seafood may be purchased.

Why the Sea is Salty

The Danish King, Frodi, when on a visit to the King of Sweden, bought two thrallwomen, Fenia and Menia, who were possessed of great strength. About the same time he was presented by a certain Hengikjoptr ('Hanging Chops'), of the giant race, with a massive quern or hand-mill called Grotti which had mysteriously turned up in Denmark, and which has the magic power of grinding out whatever it was told to grind.

So massive were the quernstones, however, that none but Fenia and Menia were able to turn the mill, and Frodi kept them incessantly at work, grinding out gold for himself.

Enraged by such treatment the bondwomen at last rebelled. As they worked they sang a song — the Quern-Song or Grotta-Song — and before it was done they had ground out an army of warriors to overthrow their oppressor.

The following night a sea-king called Mysing led them against Frodi, killing him and carrying off a pile of booty. Then they sailed away, taking the quern and the bondwomen along with him. However, once they had escaped, Mysing ordered the unfortunate bondwomen to continue grinding, not gold this time, but salt.

At midnight they asked him if they had ground enough, but he commanded them to grind on, and they did so until the weight of the salt caused the ship to sink.

Since then, 'The Swelkie', a whirlpool in the middle of the Pentland Firth, has marked the spot where the whirling quern continues to grind salt on the sea bed.

WESTRAY'S varied terrain of hills, farmland, lochs, cliffs and sandy beaches make it attractive to a tremendous variety of birds, both resident and migrant. The village of **Pierowall** stretches along the shore in the north-east of the island, protected by hills and overlooking a sheltered bay. The bay has been a popular haven since Viking times. Indeed, 'Pirivaa' was the Vikings' second harbour in Orkney, after Kirkwall.

A large cemetery of Viking graves was discovered in the sand dunes here during the 19th century, and it was to Pierowall that the Jarl Rognvald came in 1136 at the start of his subjugation of Orkney in the wake of his sainted uncle Magnus' murder.

The present harbour at Pierowall was built recently to provide a base for boats working in the North Isles. Half a dozen seine netters work from here and the fleet is growing. The port is also used by visiting trawlers, and by a small fleet of inshore boats. A processing plant in the village, owned co-operatively, fillets and freezes fish landed there.

EDAY derives its name from the Old Norse 'Eid-ey' which means Isle of the Isthmus. It was here, on the Calf of Eday, that the pirate Gow was captured in 1725 (see Stromness). He was taken to the house of the laird, James Fea — who was, in fact, an old schoolmate — and to this day there is a bloodstain on the floor of one of the rooms which is supposed to have been left by the wounded Gow.

West of Pierowall are the ancient lands of Noltland, commanded by the Castle of the same name, which has spectacular seaward views.

Gilbert Balfour, Mary Queen of Scots' Master of the Household, ordered the castle to be built in about 1560. Along with his brothers, Balfour participated in the murder of Cardinal Beaton and was strongly suspected of complicity in the brutal murder of Darnley, the Queen's husband and thus King of Scots.

Balfour's violent life was suitably ended in execution after he was discovered in a plot to dethrone King John of Sweden.

Some five miles south-west of Westray is the flat, fertile island of STRONSAY, made famous at the end of the last century by the discovery of the body of a sea monster — 'The Stronsay Beast'. Professors travelled from all over the country to see the creature and a great debate began between scholars in Edinburgh and London about whether it was a sea monster or a shark — the latter theory being adopted by the South, the former by the North. Although no final solution was reached at the time, history has shown beyond reasonable doubt that the Beast was a large basking shark.

As early as 1319, the Privy Council records estimated that, 'the tenths of the fishing at that island, frequented then by 20 or 30 sail of the Dutch fleet . . . produced every year at a medium of about £800 Scots', and although the fishing from Stronsay dwindled in mediaeval times, it revived again during the late 19th and early 20th centuries when the island became one of the principal centres for herring curing. Evidence of the industry can still be seen in and around **Whitehall**, the only village of any size on the island, where the curing sheds are still used.

Today Whitehall has a small fleet of inshore boats, fishing lobsters, crabs and scallops. Until recently there was a fish processing plant here.

Whitehall Village

The Orkneyinga Saga records that the Jarl Rognwald attended a service in Pierowall Church, fragments of which have been incorporated into the existing church, which is a national monument.

The old well at Kilpinguie, three-quarters of a mile south of Whitehall, was once highly regarded for the medicinal qualities of its water. It was said that the water could cure anything except the Black Death.

The small island of PAPA STRONSAY lies two miles off the north-eastern corner of Stronsay, close to Whitehall. Like its neighbour, it was at one time an important centre for herring curing and there is abundant evidence of the industry around the small pier. The curers' dormitories still stand and a narrow gauge railway track runs from the pierhead to the site of the gutting and packing sheds. The latter have been replaced today by sheep pens.

Several important families had estates here, the most interesting of which are the Feas, one of whom has already been mentioned in connection with the pirate Gow. The eldest son of Patrick Fea (an ex-privateer in Charles II's reign) introduced the manufacture of kelp in 1722 — an industry which became very important in Orkney, though it ultimately proved ruinous for the islanders.

Kelp is the ash produced when certain kinds of seaweed are burned: it is an essential material in bleaching, and in soap and glass making. Most Orkney kelp was shipped to Tyneside, and the Old Statistical Account refers to kelp making in many of the coastal parishes. At the time it was one of the few ways by which an 18th century landlord might extract some profit from his island estate, and many landowners made considerable sums of money from the industry.

Indeed, until 1832 the manufacture of kelp was profitable for all concerned, but that year the industry collapsed — the direct result of import duty being removed from barilla, a cheaper alternative. Many tenants, whose livelihood depended on kelp gathering, were forced to leave Orkney, unable to scrape even the barest living, and remains of their primitive cabins may be seen still on the shores of Stronsay and elsewhere.

THE SHETLAND ISLANDS

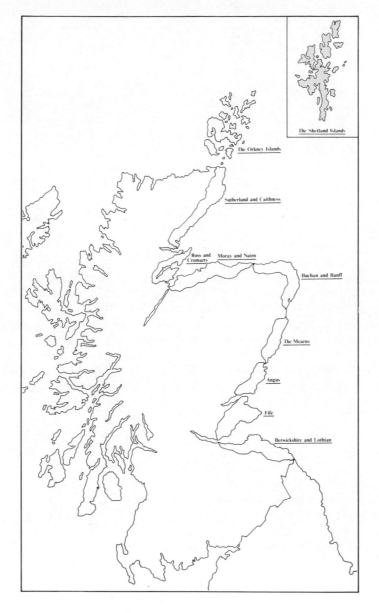

It is difficult to think of Shetland as being part of Scotland, for it has an atmosphere, character and physical presence which is unique.

In the first place, the islands are much larger than they appear on the map. There are over 100 of them — 550 square miles of land surrounded by 3,000 miles of coastline. From Sumburgh in the South Mainland to the north coast of the island of Unst is seventy miles. Yet no place is further than three miles from the sea. The islands are riven with fjords and inlets — called 'voes' in Shetland — many of which provide calm bays and safe harbours for the fishing boats which work these northern waters.

Fishing has always played an important part in the Shetlander's life. Unlike Orcadians, who have been described as 'farmers who fish', the Shetlander is 'a fisherman with a croft'. Although the southern part of the Mainland is green and fertile, the majority of the rest of Shetland is rough highland terrain, covered in heather, rock and peat bog. From earliest times the inhabitants looked to the sea for their support.

And the sea was well able to supply them. Halibut, cod, haddock, skate, ling, saithe, tusk, mackerel, whiting and herring are abundant, close to the islands, and the great northern fishing grounds towards Iceland and Norway are within striking distance.

As early as the 14th century there were signs of commercial fishing in Shetland. German merchants arrived at the islands in the month of May, set up booths on plots rented from local landowners and displayed goods such as lines and hooks, tobacco, salt, fruit, linen and alcohol — everything needed by the islanders. Local fishermen caught as many ling and cod as possible and bartered with the merchants who then had the fish salted and dried for export to Bergen, Bremen, Lubeck and Hamburg.

The boats used were called 'yoals'. Narrow in the beam and not unlike diminutive Viking longships in appearance, these boats often sailed several miles from the coast in spite of being little more than 20 ft. overall.

In 1712 a Salt Tax was introduced which subjected foreign vessels carrying salt to a very heavy duty. This had dramatic effects on Shetland. First, it killed trade with the Hanseatic merchants and, second, it obliged the local landowners to become fish merchants. Cut off from their former source of money and goods, the fishermen-crofters were unable to pay cash rents, and the only course open

Like Orkney, Shetland was part of Norway until the 15th century; the islands are equidistant between Aberdeen and Bergen; place-names, traditions and customs are Norse; even the appearance and language of the islanders owe much to Scandinavia.

It was considered wrong to mention the name of a dead person. A widow referred to her spouse as 'him 'at belonged ta me' or as 'da bairns' fayther'.

By the 16th century Dutch herring busses were taking huge catches in the seas east of Shetland. John Campbell describes the Dutch fishermen in *An Exact and Authentic Account of the Greatest White-Herring Fishery in Scotland, Carried on Yearly in the Island of Zetland, by the Dutch only* (1750):

'Now, as to the Dutch, they go to the number of ten or eleven hundred. They enter fishing upon this Coast the beginning of June, where they continue fishing till the beginning of September, during which Space they load sundry Times, carry the first to Holland, where it sells at an exorbitant Rate, seeing a hundred Dollars is reckoned but a small price for a Barrel of Herrings at Amsterdam or Rotterdam, for the first that are caught upon this Coast; . . . they send the other Loads all over Europe, up to the Mediterranean, and all over Italy, and the Italians are great Eaters of Fish, on Account of their many Lents, readily barter their Goods with the Dutch for their Herrings, the Product of our Coasts, the Profit of which must, upon a moderate Computation bring the *Dutch* in a Million Sterling annually; yea they have even the Assurance to dispose of them at our own Markets, and we are so weak as to pay them ready Money for them, so that I may justly say, the Dutch outdo us both in Industry and Prudence.'

to the landowners was to enter the trade as 'middle men'. They became boat owners, merchants and bankers, and took full advantage of the bounty of three shillings per cwt. offered to fishermen by the British Government to encourage competition with the Dutch. Larger boats known as 'sixareens' or 'sixerns' (after the number of oars they carried) were built, and fish were caught even further from shore.

Aside from those who were employed in the Merchant Navy or at the whaling — both common occupations among Shetlanders right up to modern times — the entire male population spent the months of May, June, July and August at the fishing. This was the era of the 'haaf fishing' — fishing on the open sea between forty and sixty miles from land — in frail, undecked boats rarely over 30 feet in length.

Ling, tusk and cod were sought on long-lines and conditions were hazardous. In the Old Statistical Account several ministers highlighted this: Rev. John Menzies was critical: 'They must fish for their master, who either give them a fee entirely inadequate to their labour and their dangers, or take their fish at a lower price than others would give.'

Even when the New Statistical Account was written in 1845, fishing was still a condition of land occupancy.

'The island of *Zetland*, vulgarly called *Shetland*, formerly belonged to Norway: But *James* the third of *Scotland*, having married a Princess of *Denmark*, this, with the Orkney Islands, were given him in *Portion* with her: It lies distant N.E. from *Johnny Groot's House*, commonly called the *World's End*, in Caithness, about 40 Leagues. . . .''

(John Campbell, 1750)

'Their chief Occupation, (I mean the Common People) is Fishing, and making coarse Stockings, and a kind of Woollen Cloth, called Shag, which they wear themselves . . . in the Summer, the Men are obliged to go to sea a fishing for Cod and Ling for the Lord of the Mannor . . . in the Beginning of Summer, there is as great a Bustle in getting Men go to Sea to fish the whole Summer, for these Masters, as there is here, comparatively, when we are at War with France or Spain, to find men to send Abroad; yet these Masters are as absolute as some Princes, for if these poor People do but murmur in the least at their Orders, they and their Families are banished for ever out of their Territories.'

(John Campbell, 1750)

'Tea is a luxury but rarely enjoyed. Their living consists of, in the morning, *thick porridge*, oatmeal boiled in an iron pot until it is thick. This being poured into a large bowl, each being provided with a large horn spoon, they sit round, all eating out of the same vessel; to flavour which, they, generally, have a little curdled sour milk, but some prefer a little fresh milk. The second meal is not, generally, until 4 or 5 o'clock, when they boil a pot full of potatoes and fish, which when the weather will permit, they have fresh every day; but, if not, they have fish dried in the *air*, called *vivda*, which is of a sour tainted taste. The potatoes and fish are then poured into a wooden trough, about two feet long, and about half that wide, which is placed on a stool. They all sit round the trough. The women and children skin the potatoes with their fingers, and *eat with the same*; the men, frequently, have a pocket knife, called a *jockerleg*, with which they peel theirs, and eat their fish in their hand. They eat nothing but unleavened bread, and their common beverage is *bland*, a sort of whey mixed with water and kept till it ferments and is sour. They have seldom more than two meals a day. . . . The beds in which they sleep rather differ. Some of them are above one another, in a corner, like large broad shelves. The first boards are placed near the floor, and then about two or three feet above, there is a second shelf. I have seen a third above that. On these boards they lay loose straw, or dried seaweed, with a blanket over the straw, and a blanket and rug above it; so that in this small space a whole family will sleep. The children at the bottom, the master and mistress in the middle, and the old mother, or sisters, &c., at the top.'

The History of the Shetland Isles,
Rev. James Catton (1838)

In the 1790s a number of larger smacks — ketches and tops'l schooners — had begun to fish even further afield, and when a sudden storm in 1832 sank 31 sixareens, drowning 105 men, many more larger boats were built.

By the 1840s there was a small fleet of smacks deep-water fishing around the Faroes, Rockall and Iceland, and in the Davis Straits. This lasted until the 1880s, by which time steam trawlers had arrived, capable of netting huge quantities of fish, and thus disrupting the grounds and depressing the market. Many deep-water fishermen turned to the rapidly growing herring industry.

As early as the 1820s a number of Shetland fishermen had purchased half-decked boats with which to fish herring. So many of these were wrecked in a storm in the 1840s that the Shetland Bank collapsed, but during the 1870s a second attempt was made to establish a herring fishery. Important centres grew up on the south and west coasts, especially at Scalloway, Skeld, Whiteness and Weisdale; Lerwick became a base for merchants associated with the fishing and Voe provided facilities in the north.

By 1905 more than half the entire Scottish herring catch was landed in Shetland. The following year herring auctions started in Lerwick. Smaller stations shut down and fishing became concentrated on Baltasound, Lerwick, Sandwick and Scalloway.

The collapse of the fishing industry in Shetland was dramatic. The activities of Norwegian whalers were given most of the blame, although it is more likely that the herring shoals simply changed their movements. The First World War disrupted the traditional Continental markets and many men did not return to keep the fisheries alive, yet in spite of this there was still a substantial industry until the advent of the purse-seine net.

In recent years, the oil industry has arrived in Shetland. Sullum Voe, in the northern Mainland, is a major terminal for the North Sea. Yet the industry is well contained. Even bays and inlets within sight of the flaring towers and storage tanks of Sullum Voe remain as they have been for decades, and one of the few obvious signs of the industry is the excellent road which now runs from Lerwick to the north coast.

Fishing in Shetland is not nearly as prosperous as it was formerly. The grounds are depleted, quotas are imposed by distant governments, and the Shetlanders — a race of fishermen — resent having so little control over their own destiny. All over the islands there are voes and beaches formerly used by fishermen. Forty-five of such places have been remarked upon in this section, and to do this the islands have been roughly divided into three parts: the Central and South Mainland, the West Mainland, and the North Mainland and (Northern) Isles.

THE CENTRAL AND SOUTH MAINLAND

The wide, sheltered waters of Bressay Sound have been a haven to seafarers for centuries. It was here King Hakon of Norway harboured his 120 longships in 1263 while on his way to the final test of strength with the King of Scots which ended in the Battle of Largs: it was here that another Norse king, Harald Hardrada, sheltered prior to meeting King Harald of England at Stamford Bridge in 1066.

The first fishermen to make use of the anchorage were the Dutch in the 16th century. Fleets of herring busses crowded the Sound, and brought with them traders and merchants who set up their booths and stalls on the shore.

This was the beginning of **Lerwick**, Shetland's principal town, and by the end of the 17th century about 300 families lived there.

Lerwick

he sixareen was nsurpassed for long-ne fishing and emained the principal ashore craft until the 930s. A number of oatyards in Shetland ill build them.

Shetland fishes or she ies.' (Local proverb)

All halibut caught were ept for the fishermen nd their families as hey could not be alted.

105

In 1567 the Earl of Bothwell, fleeing from Scotland, called at Shetland en route to Norway. He chartered a German merchant's ship, the *Pelikaan*, and set sail. His pursuers almost caught him in Bressay Sound for as the *Pelikaan* sped out of the north entrance, the *Unicorn*, commanded by Sir William Kirkcaldy, sailed in the south entrance. Fortunately for Bothwell he had a local pilot who cleverly steered the *Pelikaan* close to a sunken rock a few miles north and the pursuing vessel, trying to follow the same course, struck the rock and sank. The reef is still known as the Unicorn Rock.

The potential of Bressay Sound was realised by the British Government and in 1653, 94 English ships anchored there and landed troops to fortify the Sound and deny its use to the Dutch. The troops stayed for only three years and left Fort Charlotte as their memorial.

In the 18th century Shetland became a centre for the export of dried fish, butter and knitted stockings to North Germany. Smuggling also played an important part in the early trade of the islands: the merchants of Lerwick each had a private jetty with a storehouse designed for the concealment of contraband. When the cod fishing began in the Faroes, smuggling increased, and meanwhile the friendly Dutchmen kept the islanders supplied with cheap tobacco, brandy and gin, as they had done for centuries.

Until 1845 there was no road across Shetland, and curers' supplies from Lerwick had to be transported fifty miles by sea, round the stormy headlands of Sunburgh and Fitful. Alternatively the supplies were carried overland on the backs of men, women and sturdy Shetland ponies.

Smuggling was so well developed during the 19th century that contraband from Europe was even carried to London. Ships leaving Lerwick, bound for England, would obtain customs clearance for a coastal journey only. They would then leave U.K. waters, load up with taxable foreign goods and complete their voyage as if they had merely been held up by bad weather.

Throughout the 19th century the citizens of Lerwick watched the flurry of activity every March as the Greenland whalers called to complete their crews. Shetlanders were esteemed by the whaling companies for their skill and experience in handling small boats. Furthermore, the activities of the press gangs in England made whalers scarce. The whalers stayed for ten or twelve days during which the crews sought entertainment ashore and local men thronged the agents' offices seeking berths. However, the landowners, whose living depended on their tenants fishing, penalised the relatives of men who signed up for the whaling.

The last Greenland whaling ship to recruit a crew at Lerwick arrived in 1911, but the islanders' involvement in the whaling industry ceased only with the selling of Salvesen of Leith's last factory ship in the 1960s.

Sir Robert Stout

Born in Lerwick in 1844, Stout emigrated to New Zealand as a young man. He taught for several years, studied law, and in 1884 became Prime Minister of his adopted country.

On the 4th August 1814, Sir Walter Scott landed at Lerwick, a 'weary, wet and sea-sick minstrel', as he described himself in a letter to the Duke of Buccleuch. His arrival coincided with the return of the Greenland-men and the streets were 'full of drunken, riotous sailors'. He remarked that 'the Zetlanders themselves do not get drunk, but go straight to their homes and reserve their hilarity for the winter season when they spend their wages in dancing and drinking'.

The fishermen often held parties, known as 'foys', at the end of the fishing season. The chief toast was not the reigning monarch but was of more personal significance:
"Death to the head that wears no hair,
In Guid had his haand aboot da cuts."

The development of the herring fishery was the catalyst for the expansion of Lerwick, after 1878. Boats and fishermen were only a small part of the activity around the harbour. The herring had to be gutted, cured and packed: the boats and equipment had to be maintained and ships arrived daily discharging wood from the Baltic, salt from Spain and coal from the Tyne, and reloading with cargoes of salt herring for Germany and the Baltic. By the 1890s Lerwick was the major herring port in Great Britain — boats came from Ireland, the Isle of Man, the Hebrides and the whole east coast of Britain between Wick and Lowestoft. Dutchmen, Danes, Swedes and Finns made Lerwick their base at weekends. Such was the crush on the streets that even in the 1920s and '30s notices reading 'Keep Left' were posted on the pavements!

Until the 1960s, when EEC fishing limits were imposed, the town was busy with foreign fishermen. There are slightly less today, but still Norwegians, Germans, Dutch and Swedish sailors mingle with Canadian and American oil men on the quayside of Lerwick.

The older parts of Lerwick are particularly attractive with buildings fashioned from local sandstone, each displaying individual characteristics. At the water's edge the storehouses still reach out into the sea, and at the southern end of the town some of these have been well restored. Not far from the Town Hall, at the Lower Hillhead, is the Shetland Museum which covers all aspects of the history of the islands and, in particular, the fishing.

Scalloway, Shetland's second largest town, is only six miles from Lerwick. It is much older than the latter, but unlike the capital grew very slowly, suffering not a few setbacks in the course of its development.

The name derives from the Norse 'Skalavagr', the bay of the 'Skali' or hall. The only 'hall' apparent today is the ruinous pile of Scalloway Castle, built in 1600 by Earl Patrick Stewart. 'Tall and gaunt but not without grace', the castle stands on a promontory dividing Scalloway from East Voe and dominates the whole area. Its builder removed the law court there from Tingwall, where the Assembly had sat since Viking times, but he was executed fifteen years later and in time the court was moved to Lerwick.

In 1700 there were still less than 100 residents and throughout the 18th century the village stagnated: in 1797, Scalloway was described as having 'fallen much into decay'. Then, in 1820, one Charles Nicholson built a number of full decked smacks for the distant cod fishing. The town began to

In 1642 Marion Pardoun was burned at the stake in Scalloway. Twenty charges of witchcraft were found proven. Among other things she was charged with assuming the form of a porpoise and capsizing a boat, then drowning and devouring the four occupants. It was also claimed that while she was going from Brecon to Hillswick the devil appeared to her in the likeness of two crows which hopped alongside her on the way. She pleaded that the reason they had followed her was that she had fed them crumbs of bread but of course this was disbelieved.

The last witches to be burned at Scalloway were Barbara Tulloch and her daughter, Ellen King, put to death in 1712.

grow. Blackness pier was built in the 1830s and then came the herring industry, and by the turn of the century Scalloway was the major centre for the early herring fishing. Curers, packers and dryers all set up there: increasing trade encouraged cargo vessels to come direct from Leith; roads were built, connecting the growing town with Lerwick; a school and a church were established.

Scalloway

Certain people were considered unlucky if they were 'met with' on the way to the fishing. Other — those with a 'guid fit' — were welcomed.

By the turn of the 20th century Scalloway had important trade connections with Germany which imported large quantities of lightly cured matje herring: by the 1920s kippered herring from the town had a wide reputation.

'There are little Horses in this Island, which the Inhabitants call Shelties, they are so very small that one may lay his leg over them from the Ground; but notwithstanding their Smallness, they are both strong and active, and live many Years.'

(John Campbell, 1750)

During the Second World War, Scalloway was chosen as a base for the Norwegian Resistance. Patriots would regularly cross to German-occupied Norway in small fishing boats to land ammunition and saboteurs and return with refugees. The Prince Olav Slipway at the west end of the village commemorates a visit by the present King of Norway in 1942.

In recent years the dock and harbour at Scalloway have been reconstructed and today the port provides a base for about 20 trawlers and seine netters. There is a large modern fish market and fish processing is a major industry: there are three fish processing factories in the village and shipments of frozen fish are exported direct from here to the USA. The town has the largest boatyard in Shetland, and one of its three slipways is capable of

Fishermen wore bulky sheepskin coats and wide leather boots when at sea; the father of each family wore a red woollen cap which tapered to a point. Rivlins, fashioned out of untanned hide or sealskin, were worn on the feet.

taking ships as big as the ferries which ply between the islands.

West of Scalloway lie the islands of TRONDRA and BURRA now connected to the mainland by bridges. Burra itself is really two thin islands, West Burra and East Burra. By Shetland standards they are densely populated.

From Norse times until the early 19th century the people of Burra lived by the sea. They had a reputation for independence and were known for their expertise and stamina. Thus, they were among the first Shetlanders to go to the cod fishing off the Faroe Islands and with the decline of the cod fishing they pioneered the herring fishery with the first herring smack in Shetland, *The Lass o' Gowrie*. Still today, most of the crews working out of Scalloway are Burra men.

Hamnavoe, in the northern part of West Burra, is the largest village on the island. It grew up as a fishing village around an excellent natural harbour — a small inlet in an exposed headland. Since the building of the bridges in 1970 Hamnavoe has become a popular place to commute to Lerwick from.

KRAPPIN

1 large cod's head
1 lb fish liver
¼ lb fine oatmeal
seasoning

Break up the fish liver with the fingers and mix it with a similar amount of fine oatmeal and flour. Season with salt and pepper and continue mixing until the mixture holds together and forms a ball. The head should be washed carefully, and the gills and any blood removed. Then, it should be packed with the oatmeal and liver mixture and boiled in salted water for 20-30 minutes. Serve with hot potatoes.

Hamnavoe

Nearly every creek and inlet in Burra harbours boats of one sort or another, many of them built to traditional designs, and many of them used for fishing as well as pleasure. On one of these creeks is the hamlet of **Papil** which was once an important curing centre. There is no pier at Papil today, but the place is full of charm, with its cluster of houses clinging to a small promontory and overlooking a sheltered bay.

It was in Papil kirkyard that the 'Papil Stones' were found. The simpler of the two, known as the 'Monk's Stone', depicts a procession of hooded figures, one on horseback, and is today in the Shetland Museum; the other, heavily decorated in a Pictish style, is in the National Museum of Antiquities in Edinburgh.

> As in many of the east coast fishing villages, the act of pushing a boat off the beach had to be done in a particular way. The boat had to be turned 'sungaets', with the sun, and never 'widdergaets', in the opposite direction. This may have been a relic of sun worship.

Burra's counterpart on the east side of the mainland is WHALSAY, one of the most densely populated of the Shetland islands (over 1,000 souls) and one of the few remaining places very largely dependent on fishing for survival.

The main village on Whalsay is **Symbister**, with a fine sheltered harbour and a sizeable fish processing plant which prepares mainly haddock and whiting for the American market. That the village has long been connected with fishing is evidenced by the ruined Pier House, a building which dates from the days of the Hanseatic trade.

> An 'expert' was often required to inspect the boards of a new boat before sailing. The expert could foresee any tragedy by studying the grain of the wood and the knots. Swirling shapes resembling wind or waves indicated misfortune. Knots shaped like fish revealed the prospects of good catches.

The SKERRIES are a cluster of tiny islands lying some eight miles north-east of Whalsay. The entire group is barely a square mile in extent, yet it has always been an important fishing station, being closer to the rich northern grounds, and in spite of being so small the islands still support a hundred souls whose livelihood is fishing, but who also have small agricultural holdings.

The two longest islands in Skerries are connected by a bridge, and there have been curing stations and drying beaches on **Housay**, the larger of the two, for hundreds of years. Today it has a small fish processing factory, and the excellent, almost landlocked, harbour is busy with boats of all sizes.

After the Dutch ship *Kennemerlandt* was wrecked in 1664, a huge amount of spirits was recovered and it was recorded that the inhabitants were in a state of intoxication for the next 20 days.

> The first settlers from Norway brought many superstitions with them and some of these beliefs clung on till the late 19th century.
>
> The trows (trolls) were believed to be little folk who lived underground. They were happy people, fond of music and good food. Yet the people feared them and called them 'da guid folk' in order not to offend any who might be listening. The people believed that the trows carried off their children and best animals and left in their place perfect replicas ('changelings') which were ailing or died within a few days.
>
> It was said that the trows left Whalsay around 1850 when fishermen at sea noticed a great disturbance ashore 'more like soldiers at drill than anything else . . .'.
>
> It was also said in Unst that the trows felt compelled to leave their homes because they could not stand the preaching of Dr Ingram, the famous Free Kirk minister who died in 1879.

Until the lighthouse was built in 1852, the Skerries claimed many ships. In 1711, a fleet of ships left Amsterdam bound for Batavia and Ceylon by the faster northern route. One of the fleet, *De Liefde*, came to grief on the Skerries. On Sunday, 7th November, after church, the islanders discovered a solitary bewildered Dutchman stumbling about. He was the sole survivor of *De Liefde* and explained that he had been on lookout and thrown onto land when the ship struck. In 1965 there was a successful attempt to locate the wreck and, in 1967, 4,000 silver coins were recovered along with other important finds.

The Out Skerries are the most easterly point of the Shetland Isles: the most southerly point is Sumburgh Head, and the island's principal airport is situated near here, some 25 miles from Lerwick. Close by is **Grutness**, the terminal for the small ferry boat that serves Fair Isle once a week in winter, twice in summer.

> Jarlshof, close to Grutness, is one of the most famous, and most remarkable, archaeological sites in Britain. The sites appears to have been continuously inhabited for over 3,500 years, from about 2000 BC to the 16th century. Around an Iron Age broch cluster the remains of circular stone huts, two 'wheelhouses' dating from the 6th and 7th centuries, a Norse farmstead (early 9th century), a mediaeval farmstead and the Laird's 'new hall' built in the 16th century. The site was named 'Jarlshof' by Sir Walter Scott in his novel *The Pirate*.

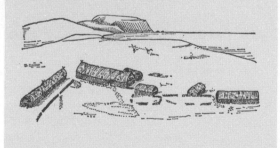

Inshore saithe fishing from Grutness Voe is recorded in the Sagas, and continued right up to this century. The yoals worked the fast-flowing tidal waters close inshore below Sumburgh Head and caught fish on hand lines. Later the village became an important curing station.

Notices on the present pier forbid the gutting of fish — an indication that Grutness is still active as a fishing centre — and on the pierhead is a substantial new shed for storing gear.

Eastshore has a substantial pier on the tidal pool of Virkie, the voe above Grutness Voe. The Ness Boating Club has its headquarters on the pierhead and organises a series of sea angling competitions. In the voe below the straggling village of **Boddam**, two and a half miles further north, is a tiny stone and cement pier. There, a roofless gear shed and an old winch above the shingle beach are the only indications that boats were once based here: archaeological remains in the area — such as Clumlie Broch, a half mile to the north — suggest

that Boddam Voe has provided shelter to fishing boats for many hundreds of years.

The whole shore below **Cumlewick** was built up with curing yards at the end of the last century — 20 or 30 at the station's height — and the area was known as 'Broonies Taing' after the little peninsula on which the stone pier was built.

Boats landed their catches on narrow jetties below the individual yards, and larger vessels — square riggers from Holland and Germany mainly — would load with cured fish for the Continental market.

Still alive in the village is an old man who can remember the whole bay encompassed by Cumlewick Ness and Levenwick Ness full of ships at anchor, waiting for wind to take them across the North Sea.

The southern part of Shetland contains some of the best agricultural land in the islands and is today best known for its farming industry. Earlier this century, however, the men of the south combined farming with fishing for herring and saithe in summer. **Aith Voe** in Cunningsburgh District, once an important centre for herring curing, is now crammed with small pleasure boats in summertime. Near the small jetty is a herring boat, at least 80 years old, which, upturned, has made an attractive store; on the beach are the weathered ribs of two more fishing boats, evidence of the past.

the 19th century illicit andy and tobacco ere smuggled into evenwick by obliging utchmen.

1603 a Cunnings-urgh man was accused using the church there a cow byre.

Buttered Sillocks

Sillocks are the fry of the saithe or coal fish.

Sillocks, salt, oatmeal, butter.

'The perfect dish of sillocks must be caught and cooked by the consumers. When the moon rises on a late summer's night, you must fish far out on a sea moved only by the slow, broad Atlantic swell. And the little mountain of sillocks, the reward of cold but exciting hours, must be "dite" (cleaned) in a moonlit rockpool. Then home at cockcrow.

'Around the kitchen fire, while the rest of the household sleep, come the happy rites of cooking and eating. Each tiny, headless fish, wrapped in a stout jacket of salted oatmeal, is popped into a pan of hot butter. There they bounce and spit while fishers, ringed round pan and fire, exquisitely thaw. At last, richly browned and curled into fantastic shapes, and so tender they almost fall to pieces, they are dished.

'Sillock-eating at the kitchen table dispenses with knives and forks. You lift a sillock gently between thumb and forefinger, snip off the tail, press the plump sides — and the backbone shoots forth! The delicious morsel left — hot, crisp oatmeal and sweet, melting fish — you eat on buttered "bere" bread, a darkly brown, flatly sour scone.'

(*The Scot's Kitchen*, F. M. McNeill)

THE WEST MAINLAND

The soft green hills of the south are in stark contrast to the rugged, heather-covered mass of the West Mainland of Shetland.

The area designated as 'The West' is a peninsula, eight miles from east to west and about six miles north-south at its widest point. Pocked with locks, riven with voes (at its narrowest part, between Aith Voe and Bixter Voe, it is a mere two miles), and corrugated with craggy hills, it has a number of harbours, particularly on its northern coast.

The most southerly harbour in the West Mainland is **Skeld**, an important base for the distant water cod fishing throughout the 19th century. A relic of these days is the old sail loft close to the pier. After declining for several years, Skeld is now making a comeback as a sea angling centre, and there is a small fleet of part-time creel boats and a large new seine-netter based there.

The only port of any size on the southern coast of the peninsula is **Walls**, built around a fine natural harbour. It has a deep water quay — the mainland terminal for the small ferry boat that serves the people of Foula, 18 miles out in the Atlantic and the loneliest inhabited island in Northern Europe — frequently used by the boats from Scalloway and Burra which put in for a night's rest while fishing west of Scotland.

At the head of the voe is the village proper, dominated by Bay Hall, a large 18th century edifice built by a successful merchant close to the old stone pier.

At the west entrance of the voe of Walls, on the island of Voisa, Arthur Anderson established the Shetland Fishery Co. in 1838. The S.F.C. was an attempt to break the hold of the landowners on the fishing. Essentially it was a co-operative and it was successful for a time, until the market failed. The remains of several small jetties still run into the bay west of the pier and there are signs of the curing sheds which formerly stood above them. Ships from Aberdeen and Leith called here and boats fishing the Faroes and Greenland seas used Walls as a base.

> Arthur Anderson was a remarkable man. In the late 18th century he was impressed into the Royal Navy. Once discharged, he took a job as a clerk with a shipping company in London, and after marrying the owner's daughter, built up the company and changed its name to Pacific & Orient (P. & O.). He was a great philanthropist and sat as M.P. for Orkney and Shetland for many years.

The north coast of the West Mainland, facing St Magnus Bay, has some of the most spectacular scenery in the whole of Shetland. At its easternmost is the village of **Sandness**, with its little harbour at Melby. From here there is an excellent view of the island of PAPA STOUR, beyond which lies the Vee Skerries, the graveyard of many fine ships including the Aberdeen trawler *Ben Doran*, wrecked there in 1930 with the loss of all hands.

One body was interred at Sandness churchyard where the *Ben Doran* memorial now stands. Following this tragedy, the R.N.L.I. opened its most northerly station at Aith (see below).

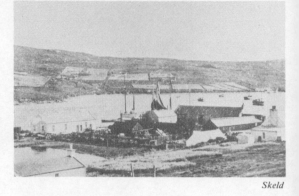

Skeld

West Burrafirth, two miles east of Sandness, is sheltered in all weathers and was formerly a sizeable herring station with a wooden, and later stone, pier.

At the time of writing, this stone pier is being substantially enlarged to accommodate the car ferry to Papa Stour, and this will undoubtedly encourage more boats to adopt West Burrafirth as a base. At the moment the harbour is used by a number of boats working off Papa Stour and the Voe Skerries and provides a base for half a dozen creel boats, all under 32 feet in length.

> It was believed that if a silver coin bearing the head of Charles I was placed on a boil, it would cure it. The coin was put in boiling water first and would draw the poison. It was called 'da kruel coin' because boils were known as 'kruels'. There is one such coin in the Shetland Museum.

Aith Voe, further east, is long and broad, and at its head is the village of **Aith** itself. Four boats are based here all year round — along with a number of part-timers — and two or three more in the summer months. The fishing is mainly for queen scallops in the well-stocked waters of Aith Voe and East Burrafirth.

After the *Ben Doran* disaster in 1930, a lifeboat station — the most northerly in the British Isles — was built at Aith to cover the west coast of Shetland. In the 55 years of its service, Aith lifeboat has saved numerous lives, and the village is shortly to take delivery of a new Arran Class lifeboat.

THE NORTHERN MAINLAND AND THE ISLES

The northern half of the mainland of Shetland is deeply indented with voes and inlets. Some of them run inland for miles, like Norwegian fjords, and others, such as Sullom Voe, have become household names on account of the oil industry. The road to Sullom Voe passes the attractive village of **Voe**, built at the head of a long fjord. Although it has no fleet of its own today, Voe was once a major centre for the deep water cod fishing, and is still used by vessels operating in St Magnus Bay. The village is very picturesque. A cluster of sturdy stone cottages with corrugated iron roofs huddle round the pier, at the head of which are several old sheds, now converted, and a small boat-yard. The harbour is popular with pleasure boats and has two full-time scallop boats.

Just north of Voe, but on the east coast, is the thriving fishing village of **Vidlin**. The village looks out over its own voe — a bay crowded with salmon cages, for Vidlin is the largest salmon station in Shetland. About 100,000 fish are farmed here and processed in the large new shed to the south of the bay.

Until recently, Vidlin was also an important centre for lobsters. Few lobsters are caught off Shetland today, and the shellfish formerly kept in the large lobster pond were imported from Orkney and held until the price was right. The village also had at least one trawler devoted entirely to fishing for sand eels. This fishery is still vigorous, and is increasing elsewhere. Over-fishing with large nets has greatly reduced the numbers of fish which prey on the eels, and accordingly the latter are now found in unprecedented numbers. No sand eels are sought from Vidlin today and the only boats working from here are small craft after scallops.

Lunna, two miles further north, has a small stone jetty still used by fishing vessels, although its chief moment of glory came during the Second World War when the harbour was used by Norwegian Resistance fighters as they carried on their war against the Germans.

To reach **Mossbank** by road, one is obliged to back-track to Voe and rejoin the main road which is the spine of the mainland.

The first evidence of the oil boom is apparent in the cluster of new houses above Voe, and the area around Mossbank — some ten miles further north — has been extensively built on to provide houses for oil personnel. There are even streetlights along the road between Mossbank and its nearest neighbour, Northlee.

Mossbank itself was formerly a fishing community and in 1904 suffered the tragic loss of four boats and 22 men, leaving behind them 15 widows and 61 dependants.

Ness Yoal

Sullom Voe is the largest voe in Shetland, almost severing the north-western corner of the mainland. The oil terminal named after the voe spreads itself over the barren hillside of Caldback to the north-west in a town of tanks, towers and pipelines. Crude oil from the North Sea is brought ashore here in huge 48-inch pipes and stored before being shipped in tankers to destinations all over the world for refining.

Collafirth

The former fishing station of **Graven** is 'in the shadow' of the terminal. The harbour here used to be indispensable to fishermen working Yellsound and fish is still landed, although most of the new piers and slipways that have been built in recent years are for other vessels.

Ollaberry is a picturesque spot, with wild hills behind, its own small bay and an attractive little church close to the village slipway.

There was a herring station here until the 1930s, and fishing is in the blood of the people. Four or five boat crews live in the village — although they work out of other ports, including the crews of one of the largest purse seine-netters in Britain, the *Altaire*.

Collafirth is two and a half miles further north, a broad and lonely bay with a little, sheltered voe — the Voe of the Brig — in its north-western corner. The pier here is made of wood and is badly decayed, and this sad remnant is all that remains of a once prosperous Norwegian whaling station and a herring curing yard which operated until the 1930s. In spite of its unsafe condition, fishermen still risk the rotting boards to land fish here. The situation of Collafirth is ideal for boats working in northern waters: there is a good depth of water at the pier and trucks collect catches for transportation to Lerwick. There has been more than one petition for the repair of the pier, and it is to be hoped that before long something will be done to restore this useful little harbour.

Four and a half miles north again is **North Roe**, once a major herring station, but little used today. In 1907 the people of North Roe, along with the rest of Shetland, became involved in a dispute about the Norwegian whalers. The fishermen protested that the whaling would kill off the herring industry, and the crofters complained about the pollution—once stripped of blubber, the whale carcasses were dumped in the sea, often coming ashore to spoil the beaches. There were demonstrations and an appeal to Mr Asquith, the Prime Minister. However, there was unemployment in the islands and as the Norwegian whaling stations employed up to 100 men each, nothing was done. By 1928 the whaling industry in the islands was finished.

In the most northern tip of the mainland are two of the most interesting spots in the whole of Shetland: the ruined haaf fishing stations of **Stenness** and **Fedeland**. The latter was a small crofting township and can be reached only after a two-mile walk from Isbister, but it is well worth the effort, for the landscape is stunning and much of the vegetation, growing in volcanic soil, is Alpine.

Penetrating deep into the North Mainland from the west is **Ronas Voe**, a fjord-like inlet overshadowed by the red granite mass of Ronas Hill — at 1,476 feet the highest in Shetland.

> In December 1674, during the Anglo-Dutch War, the man o' war *Het Wapen van Rotterdam* came to shelter in the deep water of Ronas Voe. The British promptly sent two frigates to blockade the voe and overpower her crew. The Dutch sailors who were killed in the skirmish were buried on the southern shore of the voe and the site is still known as 'Hollanders' Grave'.

Ronas Voe is used by ships of several nationalities during bad weather. Halfway up the voe, on its southern shore, is a stone pier marked on the chart as Skeo Head. There is one full-time trawler based here, and others land fish during the summer, to supply the substantial processing plant close by. Cod, haddock and whiting are all filleted and frozen, and then transported to Scalloway or Lerwick for shipment. The factory has been running since 1973.

A mile west of Skeo Head pier is **Heylor** pier, where the remains of a Norwegian whaling station, dating from 1904, can be seen. There are also signs showing that Heylor was a herring station.

The island of YELL to the north-east of the mainland is the least fertile of all the inhabited islands of Shetland, covered with peat and grazed by small Shetland sheep and cattle. Because of the poverty of the land, the inhabitants of Yell had to devote themselves to surviving from the sea. Mercifully the deep coastal waters of Yellsound are rich in white fish, shellfish and halibut.

Haaf fishing was pursued from **Gloup** until a sudden storm on the night of 20th July 1881 put an end to it. Today the narrow, steep-sided northern

To burn sillocks' bones was to invite bad luck: 'Boil me and fry me but burn me no beens An' ye sal never want me aboot da eel staves'. A rhyme similar to this, with the accompanying superstition, existed in several villages in Angus and the Mearns.

voe is almost deserted.

Whalfirth, a broad voe seven miles south of Gloup, had several herring stations at the end of last century, as had **Cullivoe**, to the south-east. Here there were a dozen herring curing yards and with Whalsay, Cullivoe was the last place at which herring was cured outside Lerwick. Shellfish and white fish boats still operate from the sheltered bay.

Mid Yell itself — the largest village on the island — is an active fishing port. Half a dozen trawlers are based here during the season, and others land fish for the two processing plants.

Baltasound

The present population of UNST lives mainly in the east of the island; at **Uyeasound**, **Baltasound**, **Haroldswick** and **Norwick**. The tradition of fishing has recently vanished; the inhabitants live by crofting and there is some quarrying for serpentine and talc, but the principal employer on the island is the R.A.F., who have an important early warning station on the island.

Yet Baltasound was once the largest herring port in Britain, replaced only by Lerwick when steam replaced sail: 'a recurrent scene of splendid and picturesque activity as the fishing fleet, filling the narrow bay with its dark brown sails, jockeyed for position. . . .' The remains of the old herring stations can be seen on both sides of the voe. It has an excellent harbour and is much frequented today by vessels of several nationalities — cargo boats loading with minerals and vessels working for the oil industry as well as fishing boats.

Lerwick Harbour, 1900s

While at sea, the fishermen talked of the weather, fishing grounds and the catch, but they avoided referring to people, animals and objects on land. A vocabulary developed which was solely used at sea. A cow was referred to as 'a boorik', a horse as 'a russi', a dog as 'a rakki', a pig as 'a hirki' and rabbits were known as 'kyunnin'.

Uyeasound at the south end of the island has a fine little harbour which shelters a variety of small craft. At the other end of the island, **Burrafirth** is a long inlet, exposed to northerly winds, but well sheltered from other quarters and much used as an anchorage. Offshore lie the rocks of Muckle Flugga (crowned by an important lighthouse) and the isolated Out Stack, the most northerly point on the British Isles.

'I do not remember any Frost or Snow in Shetland; if any, it was not of long continuance; the coldest weather is by reason of great winds in the Winter-quarter, the wind blowing so violent, that no Ship dare look on the North Coast; so that the people of those Islands have little commerce with other Nations in that Quarter. I can speak by experience. Being blown down flat to the ground by the violence of the wind, I was forced to creep on my hands and knees to the next wall, and going by the wall got into an house, or else must have stayed by the wall till the violence of the Wind were over.'
(Captain John Smith, 1661)

113

BIBLIOGRAPHY

Principle Sources

"Fishing Boats and Fisherfolk" *Peter F. Anson 1930*

"Scots Fisherfolk" *Peter F. Anson 1950*

"Fisher Folklore" *Peter F. Anson 1965*

"Fisher Life in Scotland" *J. G. Bertram 1889*

"The Statistical Account of Scotland, 1791-99"

The New Statistical Account of Scotland, 1841-85"

"The Ordnance Gazetteer of Scotland, 1844"

"Scottish Fishing Craft" *Gloria Wilson 1965*

"Sailing Craft of the British Isles" *Roger Finch 1976*

Selected Secondary Sources

"The Berwick and Lothian Coast" *I. C. Hannah 1913*

"An Old-Time Fishing Town: Eyemouth" *McIver 1906*

"From Esk to Tweed" *Bruce Lenman 1975*

"Harbours of the Forth" *Guy Christie 1955*

"Ebb-tide" *Will Wilson 1980*

"Fisher Life, or, the Memorials of Cellardyke and the Fife Coast" *George Gourlay 1879*

"Bygone Fife from Culross to St Andrews: Traditions, Legends, Folklore and Local History of the Kingdom" *James Wilkie 1931*

"In My Ain Words — An East Neuk Vocabulary" *Mary Murray 1982*

"Tales, Legends and Traditions of Forfarshire" *Alexander Lowson 1891*

"History of Arbroath" *George Hay 1876*

"Days of Yore" *G. Hutcheson 1887*

"Description of the Coast between Aberdeen and Leith" *W. Duncan 1837*

"Fisherfolk of the North-East" *Leatham 1930*

"Portrait of the Moray Firth" *Cuthbert Graham 1977*

"The Christian Watt Papers" *David Fraser 1983*

"Scenes and Legends of the North of Scotland" *Hugh Miller 1857*

"History of Moray and Nairn" *Charles G. Rampini 1897*

"Excursion along the Gamrie Coast from Macduff to past Melrose" *an article by the Banffshire Field Club 1895*

"Moray and Nairn" (Cambridge County Geographies) *C. Matheson 1915*

"Down to the Sea: An Account of Life in the Fishing Villages of Hilton, Balintore and Shadwick" *Jessie MacDonald/Anne Gordon 1975*

"The Highlands and Islands" *Francis Thompson 1974*

"The Queen's Scotland: The Eastern Counties" *Nigel Tranter 1972*

"The Queen's Scotland: The North-East" *Nigel Tranter 1974*

"The Island Series: Orkney" *Patrick Bailey 1971*

"Orkney" *Hugh Marwick 1951*

"The Shetland Sketch Book" *William Fordyce Clark 1930*

"Shetland Traditional Lore" *J. M. E. Saxby 1932*

"The Shetland Book" *A. T. Cluness 1967*

"An Exact and Authentic Account of the Greatest White-Herring Fishery in Scotland, carried on yearly in the Island of Zetland, by the Dutch only" *John Campbell 1750*

"Fishing for the Whale" *David Henderson 1972*

"Poems and Songs of the North-East Neuk" *W. R. Melvin 1949*

"The Scot's Kitchen" *F. M. McNeill 1929*

"The Scottish Cookery Book" *Elizabeth Craig 1956*

"A Taste of Scotland" *Theodora Fitzgibbon 1970*

"The Commonsense Scots Cookery Book" *Gordon Hay 1978*

"Scottish Regional Recipes" *Catherine Brown 1981*